LAUGHTER:
LAUGH MORE LIVE BETTER

– ZAC OLUSESAN ODETUNDE –

An environmentally friendly book printed and bound in England by
www.printondemand-worldwide.com

http://www.fast-print.net/bookshop

LAUGHTER: LAUGH MORE LIVE BETTER

A catalogue record for this book is available from the British Library

ISBN 978-178456-343-1

First published 2016 by
FASTPRINT PUBLISHING
Peterborough, England.

This book is dedicated to the following:

Oluwakemi, my long-suffering wife - On the day that I told her about my plan to write a book on laughter, she responded with the longest belly laugh I have ever heard from her. It is my hope that she will laugh half as much and with me when I present her a final copy.

My daughters, Esther Tolulope and Sharon Oluwatoyin – It was their 'dad, you can do it' that kept me going at it even when serious illness almost ended my plan.

My son, Stephen Oluwatosin – He organised the manuscript into a printable form. He is not called an Information Technology guru for nothing. If only he will slow down and explain things more!

ACKNOWLEDGEMENT

My boyhood-friend, John Bamberger of 33 Stubble Close, Northampton, NN2 8DS, provided more encouragement for me than he will ever realize. Our banters produced most of the jokes in Chapter 8. The funniest jokes are his.

Special mention must be made of the 'angels' at the Royal Marsden Hospital, Fulham Road, South-West London. It will be a travesty to mention names instead of teams of staff at: the Pre-assessment Department, the Medical Day Hospital, Critical Care and 'my own wards', Burdett Coutts and Markus. Your kindness, selflessness and devotion to duty touch my heart tenderly. You all have added more life to my years and more years to my life. Of that I am very sure.

CONTENTS

FOREWORD

Anyone who has read the World Classic Arabian Nights collection would attest to its rib-cracking thriller riddles and suspense-laden stories and jokes. It is said that the stories had their origin in the court of a bloody-thirsty Persian monarch named Shahryar who killed a succession of his wives on their wedding nights until he met his match in a cunning would-be-bride named Scheherazade.

Scheherazade saved herself by telling the Shah a funny story every evening leaving each tale unfinished so that the Shah delayed her execution.

This went on, so it is said, for a thousand and one nights by which time the Shah gave up his penchant for uxoricide, the killing of one's wife or wives.

Scheherazade used the power of jokes and laughter to reverse a Shah's murderous emotions. In a somewhat similar manner, modern man, hemmed in on all sides by pressures of life, can lighten his burden by exploiting the potential of laughter and thus prolong his existence in the face of the relentless Shah-like pressures of modern living. I commend Laughter – Laugh More; Live Better to readers for its educational and practical values. Some readers may enjoy reading the book more by first reading Part 2 which is for light relief according to the author.

However, this book would make an enjoyable and informative reading regardless of what part is read first.

Professor Isaac A OGUNBIYI, OON
Department of Foreign Languages
Lagos State University
OJO, Lagos, Nigeria.

PREFACE

We do it and see and hear people do it every day. Yet mystery surrounds this human phenomenon - laughter. What is laughter? What is its origin? Why do we laugh? How do we laugh? What are the neurological factors that bring laughter about? What are the benefits of laughing? Is laughter really 'the best medicine?' The search for answers to these questions is the main motivation for writing this book.

Section One consists of two chapters. In Chapter 1, laughter is defined. Also, its origin is discussed and its links to humour and happiness are explored. Theories that underly laughter are discussed. Chapter 2 lists and describes various types of laughter. The chapter takes a cursory look at the acoustics of laughter and explores some of the factors that affect how we laugh.

In Section Two (Chapter Three), the basic anatomy of laughter is discussed. The complex neuro-biological factors that lie behind the production of laughter are described.

Section Three (Chapter Four) discusses the medical, psychological and social benefits of laughter. The use of 'scientific' studies to prove the effectiveness of laughter is critiqued.

Section Four (Chapter Five) traces the origin of the use of laughter in medical practice. It discusses the current status of laughter therapy. It also describes exercises that can improve the functioning of the muscles that initiate laughter. Ideas are given that can help the reader to laugh more.

Section Five consists of Chapters 6, 7 and 8. The three chapters contain jokes and quotes from the medical and so-called para-medical fields and from life in general. The aim of these chapters is to provide light relief, and thus, as in Chapter Five, motivate the reader to laugh.

This book does not attempt to consider laughter from a scholarly point of view. That is why a concerted effort has been made to avoid the copious use of jargon and scientific terminologies. There are some exceptions, of course. In Chapters 2 to 5, terminologies and the names of anatomical structures – muscles, bones, nerves and parts of the brain – have to be used with minimal or no explanation. The functions and actions of many of the structures named are, most of the time, explanatory.

Reading lists are provided at the ends of Chapters 1, 2, 3, 4 and 5 respectivey. These are for readers who want to know more about laughter, an intriguing and very fascinating subject.

ABOUT THE AUTHOR

I was born in Ayetoro which is in Ogun Sate in the South-western corner of Nigeria. I trained in Nigeria as a Physiotherapist as part of the rehabilitation programme that followed the Nigerian civil war which ended in 1970.

I migrated to England in 1975 and worked in the National Health Service for three decades, gaining further experience in rehabilitation through studies at Southampton University and the University of East London.

Reading and creative writing have been my passion since childhood. I have contributed many articles to medical professional journals. I have also written three short novels. 'Laughter' is my debut non-fiction book.

CHAPTER 1
WHAT IS LAUGHTER?

Collins English Dictionary's definitions of laughter are:

Noun - The action of or noise produced by laughing. The experience or manifestation of mirth, amusement, or joy.

Verb - To express or manifest emotions especially mirth or amusement typically by expelling air from the lungs in short bursts to produce an inarticulate voiced noise with the mouth open.

The dictionary gives the following as the synonyms of the word laughter: chuckling, laughing, giggling, chortling, guffawing, tittering and cachinnation.

At Dictionary.com, to laugh is defined as: to express mirth, pleasure, derision or nervousness with an audible vocal expulsion of air from the lungs that can range from a loud burst of sound to a series of chuckles and is usually accompanied by characteristic facial and bodily movements.

Macmillan Dictionary defines laugh (verb) as: to make a noise with your voice that shows that you think something is funny.

Professor Sophie Scott, Deputy Director of University College London's Institute of Cognitive

Neuroscience, proffers a more scientific definition of laughter: 'non-verbal vocalisations that are unlike speech in terms of the way that they are produced with little or no involvement of the articulators – tongue, jaw, soft palate, lips. Instead these vocalisations are dominated by the effects of changes in breath control, sub-glottal pressure, laryngeal tension and facial expressions".

Laughter is a physical reaction to an internal stimulus such as one's own thoughts or external stimuli such as, seeing something, hearing a joke or being tickled. (It is difficult to tickle oneself to laugh. Try it.)

Some factors cause uncontrollable laughter. These include diseases such as multi-infarct dementia, cancer of certain parts of the brain and agents such as nitrous oxide, the laughing gas.

Laughter has often been described as the brass ring of humour. It is mostly a result of positive emotions. However, laughter can also be a display of negative emotions such as, embarrassment, regret, apology or confusion. Some examples are: nervous laughter, cynical laughter, paradoxical laughter and evil laughter.

As mentioned above, laughter is often audible. It is produced by a series of muscle actions that lead to a flow of air in and out of the lungs through the voice box, the larynx. Variations in the strength of the contraction of laryngeal muscles produce the modulation that results.

THE ORIGIN AND PURPOSE OF LAUGHTER?

Science does not have a clear answer to this question. Anthropologists agree that laughter is common to all cultures. Neuro-scientists and psychologists claim, from their study of the mammalian brain, that laughter first appeared in mammals millions of years ago. According to these scientists, the primitive mammalian brain gradually developed mophorlogically into the primate (monkeys and apes) form and then into the hominid (homo sapiens or human) form. It was then that the development of a mind occurred. This was followed by the ability to appreciate theory, communicate through language and recognise incongruity or humour.

Drs Gervais and Wilson put forward a similar theory. Duchenne laughter, the only genuine or authentic form of laughter, developed in primates some two to four million years ago. This kind of laughter was triggered by tickling or playful fighting. It was to signify that there was no danger to the group. There a was an opportunity to explore and learn. According to Gervais and Wilson, the non-Duchenne type of laughter developed only several thousand years ago. It can be aggressive or judgemental.

Most of the theories about the origin of laughter have evolutionary roots. On the contrast, creationists attribute laughter to an almighty and all-wise spirit person, God, who endowed man with the ability to laugh. The purpose of this gift is to help man cope with and survive the adverse conditions he plunged himself into following his fall from perfection. One such proponent is Frank Sherwin, an Irish (independent) politician. He dismissed evolutionary theories of laughter as "an attempt to use spin to corrupt what God has given us". The Creation versus Evolution debate rages on!

There is no single theory that fully explains laughter. One theory may explain an aspect of laughter while it ignores or at times contradicts other aspects. That is why researchers of the subject of laughter admit that though a lot is now known about it, a lot more remains to be known. Laughter is a multi-various subject. Like an elephant that is being described by several blind men who feel different parts of it, the descriptions of the different aspects of laughter can be quite subjective. Over-arching research into all the aspects of laughter is needed to provide a better understanding of this exciting human phenomenon.

So, it is not a joke to say that animals do laugh. And, it is not just monkeys and apes that laugh. Wait for it! Scientists claim that dogs, cats and mice too laugh.

Jack Panksepp, Estonian-born American psychobiologist and neuroscientist reported on laughter in mice. He tickled mice and analysed the 'chirps' that they made. He concluded that the 'chirps' were laughter sounds. He then extrapolated that mice have a sense of humour because the tickled mice became socially-bounded to their ticklers and looked for more tickles.

Patricia Simonet, a researcher at the Sierra Nevada College in Tahoe, USA, described the 'laughing sound' elicited from dogs as 'breathy, pronounced forced exhalation that sounds to the untrained ear as normal dog pants'. Simonet played the recording of these 'pants' at an animal sanctuary. Puppies reacted playfully to them in contrast to other sounds. This, to Simonet, is an example of the recognition of the existence of laughter among dogs. According to her, you can use dog 'laugh' to invite your dog (if you have one, of course) to play by saying 'ee ee'. You draw air in to your lungs and then, as if you are receiving the Heimlich manoeuvre, exhale. As you do so, make the sound 'ee ee ee' which is dog sound and not 'hee hee hee', the sound made by humans.

Robert Provine, a behavioural neurobiologist at the University of Maryland, Baltimore, USA, while investigating the origin of laughter, tickled chimpanzees at the Yerkes Regional Primate Centre in Atlanta. He found that the chimpanzees 'produced laughter sounds'. His description of chimpanzee laughter agrees with the dog laughter described above by Simmonet. Chimpanzees make 'laughter' sounds only during expiration. Humans have improved on this, Provine asserts, as we can produce some laughter sounds during inspiration.

Provine asserts that laughter is genetically controlled. Giving credence to this are findings that children born blind and deaf do laugh, babies laugh long before they acquire speech and twins separated at birth and brought up in different environments – nurture - tend to display similar laughter characteristics - nature.

TABLE 1.1 - HUMOUR DEVELOPMENT (ADAPTED FROM VARIOUS SOURCES)

Age	Humour Response
From 0 to 4 months	Responds to light, sound and movements. Able to smile.
4 to 8 months	Laughs when physically stimulated. Recognises faces and voices.
8 months to 1 year	Laughs at toys. Distinguishes between self and others.
1 to 2 years	Displays incongruent behaviour.
2 to 4 years	Displays understanding of fantasy and make-believe. Can create own humour stimulus.
5 to10 years	Can understand riddles and jokes. Can display concrete operational thoughts.
10 years and over	Has a grasp of sophisticated jokes. Displays wit and incongruent social behaviour. Shows clear individual personality.

Age, gender and culture are some of the factors that determine why, how and how often people laugh. These factors and a few others are discussed in some detail later in this book.

According to neuroscientists, laughter is controlled via a complicated circuitry that runs through many parts of the brain. The frontal part of the cerebral cortex of the left lobe or hemisphere of the brain analyses laughter stimuli. It analyses the basic meaning of what is felt, seen or heard. The frontal part of the cerebral cortex of the right lobe or hemisphere then carries out an intellectual analysis of the stimuli to determine whether the subject gets the 'joke or not'. If the stimuli are recognised as laughter stimuli, special areas of the cerebral cortex on both sides, the motor areas, then excite muscles of the face. A smile ensues. As and when the stimuli get stronger, more muscles are excited, in the larynx, diaphragm and chest wall. Different types of laughter then occur accompanied by various types of facial and bodily movements.

If the laughter stimuli become stronger still, deeper areas of the brain are excited. These areas include the back of the brain, the occipital lobes and especially the mid-brain, the neural tissues that connect the two lobes of the brain and the spinal cord. It is thought that 'belly laughter' occurs only when laughter reaches as far down as the special nerve cells in the areas of the midbrain called the limbic system. This area is described in Chapter 4.

Laughter can be measured on a sliding scale ranging from a smile to the 'I-laughed-till-I-nearly-died' or 'I-laughed-till-I-peed-myself' type of laughter. The various intensities of the sound of laughter and laughter frequencies or acoustics are described detail in Chapter 3.

Laughter is closely related to humour. Still, humour differs from laughter. Chambers Dictionary defines humour as that which causes mirth or amusement; the quality of being funny.

Humour can be classified broadly into two categories – formal and informal humour.

Formal humour is pre-planned. Examples include, court or circus jesting, story-telling, drawing cartoons, writing satire and stand-up comedy.

Most of humour is informal. **Informal Humour** is mostly impulsive and interactive. Examples of informal humour include subtle insults or jibes such as nickname calling, pointing at a friend's slip-of-the-tongue error or a pantomime such as the feigning to shoot someone dead with a water pistol and peek-a-boo. Various other pranks also fall into this category.

Humour does not always result in laughter. An object, act or joke may lack intrinsic humour in that it does not generate stimuli that are strong enough to excite the recipient's brain. On the other hand, a person may be declared as humourless. 'He never smiles or laughs' may indicate a reduced ability to appreciate humour. This may be due to the presence of disease in certain parts of the brain of the intended recipient of humour.

There are three major theories that try to explain why we laugh:

1. THE SUPERIORITY THEORY

The main tenet of this theory is that we laugh at the misfortune of others. According to the theory, when we observe another person making a mistake, we feel superior to them and this fills us with mirth. "I would not have made such a silly error", we tend to tell ourselves.

The Superiority Theory originated from the thinking of the Greek philosopher, Plato, who lived from 428 to 347 BC. Plato was a student of another Greek (Athenian) philosopher, Socrates who lived from 470 to 399 BC. Thomas Hobbes (1588 to 1679 AD) a British philosopher, strengthened the Superiority Theory two millennia later. According to Hobbes, 'laughing to one's self, puts all the rest into jealousy and self-examination of themselves.' The TV programme 'You Have Been Framed' is based on this theory.

2. THE RELIEF THEORY

Austrian neurologist, Sigmund Freud (1856 to 1939 AD), is a chief proponent of this theory. The key point of the theory is that laughter relieves the building up of nervous tension and saves psychic energy. According to Freud, the ID is the source of aggressive (including sexual drive) impulses. The SUPER EGO suppresses these impulses. When the SUPER EGO is tricked to express (or not depress) aggressive impulses, laughter occurs.

The Relief Theory provides some explanation for the success of thrillers produced as books, plays or movies.

3. THE INCONGRUITY THEORY

This is arguably the most popular of the theories of humour or laughter. The main claim of this theory is that we laugh at things that surprise us because they seem out of place. Some examples are: the clown's big red nose, a bear walking into a pub, the chicken crossing the road, etc. Laughter ensues only when the incongruity or the unexpected is resolved. In other words, we laugh only when we 'get the joke'.

The main proponent of this theory is German philosopher, Immanuel Kant, who lived from 1724 to 1804 AD. Others are James Beattie (1735 to 1803 AD), a Scottish poet and philosopher who is thought to be the first to formally formulate the theory; Herbert Spencer (1770 to 1831 AD), an English philosopher; Arthur Schopenhauer (1788 to 1860 AD), a German philosopher and Henri-Louis Bergson (1859 to 1941 AD), a French philosopher.

In the 1970s psychologists revised Kant's original theory and propounded the Incongruity-Resolution Theory. This version of the theory lays further emphasis on the resolution of the incongruity. It stresses that not all resolved incongruities are humorous or funny.

Other Theories of Laughter have been propounded. An in-depth discussion of these theories is beyond the scope of this book. Please see Table 1.2 for a brief summary of each of these theories.

TABLE 1.2 - OTHER LAUGHTER THEORIES

Theory	Proponent/s	Description
The Misattribution Theory (1980)	Doff Zillman and Jennings Bryant	The main concept of this theory is derived from Freud's assertion that 'wit' differs from 'humour'. It tries to explain why an audience fails to identify exactly why a joke is funny. They laugh anyway – to release excess energy.
The Script-based Semantic Theory (1985)	Victor Raskin	This theory is a variant of the Incongruity theory. Its main distinction is that it concerns itself mainly with words, spoken or written as they are used to narrate punchline jokes.
The General Theory of Verbal Humour (1991)	Victor Raskin and Salvatore Attardo	This theory integrates the ideas of the Script-based Semantic theory. Whereas, the original theory deals with

		jokes. This theory deals with all humorous texts.
The Computational-Neural Theory (1992)	Igor Mikhailovich Suslov	This theory proposes a computer model of humour. It creates a complex algorithm to explain the humour effects of verbal, visual and tactile stimuli.
The Ontic Epistemic Theory (2006)	Peter Marteinson	This theory asserts that humour or laughter arises from a cognitive or epistemological impasse. A person is presented with real and unreal situations. He momentarily accepts both as real. Humour of laughter ensues when it is realised that the situations are unreal.
The Benign Violation Theory (2010)	Peter McGraw and Caleb Warren	This theory suggests that anything that threatens a person's sense of how the world should be will

		be humorous as long as the threat seems to be benign.

MAN'S SEARCH FOR FUN

According to Dr Bremmer of the Faculty of Theology and Religious Studies University of Groningen, Holland, Democritus, a Greek scientist and philosopher who lived from about 460 to 370 BC, was known as the 'laughing professor' because of 'his disposition to laugh at the stupidity of his fellow citizens'.

It was the quest for amusement that gave birth to the professional or court jester. Professional jesting became a universal phenomenon in man's history over the last 5 or 6 millennia. It spread from Greece to medieval and renaissance Europe, China, Persia, India, Japan, Russia, Africa and North America.

Jesting died in China around the 17th century AD and in Europe in the 18th century AD. However, there have been pockets of resistance to its demise. Most recent examples of its survival are among the African and American tribes. Two examples are, the Wolofs of West Africa and the Sioux of North America. A unique aspect of the functions of jesters among the African and American tribes is that the jester does not answer just to the tribal chief, but first and foremost to the tribe, the people.

The jester was usually a male dwarf, a hunchback or a person with other physical or psychological oddity. His main role was, of course, to provide amusement for his master and or the people. He, however, was to do more than sing the praise of his master. He was allowed to speak his mind and curb his master's excesses. Since he was generally of low political and social status than his master, he did not pose any threat to the master's office or power. Beatrice Otto, author of the book, Fools Are Everywhere: *The Court Jesters Around the World,* declares: 'the jester often won favour among the people who perceive him as the little man fighting the powerful'.

Is the court jester dead? Certainly not. Man's search for amusement is still alive. The court jester has metamophorsised into today's circus performer, the cartoonist, the satirist, the story teller, the musician and the stand-up comedian.

The court jester of former days served a master, an emperor, a king, a Lord of the Manor or sometimes, a prominent cleric. Today's jester serves his paymaster, the public. It is also to be noted that today's jester is not necessarily a dwarf or hunchback. He stands out mostly because of his ethnicity, race, weight or wit.

Like some ancient jesters, modern jesters enjoy celebrity status. To name a few that readily come to mind: Charlie Chaplin, Robin William, Whoopi Goldberg, Eddy Murphy, Shah Ruk Khan, Aamir Khan, Salman Khan, Shahid Kapoor, Will Smith, Lisa Kudrow and the Nollywood actress, Genevieve Nnaji.

What is the future for modern day jesters? I'll allow Beatrice K Otto (cited earlier) to answer the question: "I guess we'll always need jesters or jester types because there's always going to be a lot that deserves to be mocked or cut down to size – *until we either lose the ability to laugh* (italics are mine) or the world becomes miraculously devoid of daftness, dullness and corruption. Looking at the record so far, it'll take the extinction of the human race for that to happen."

Though it is not imminent that our world will become laughless, we seem to be laughing less. Social researchers claim that people in Britain laughed 18 minutes a day in the 1950s but for 7 minutes a day in 2013. If this claim is true, the question that arises is: 'Why are we laughing less?'

A large part of the blame for the decline in laughter can be laid at the door of modern technology. Laughter is a phenomenon that occurs mainly in group settings. Modern technology, however, often promotes activities that are performed individually. Try to talk to a teenager. You may find yourself competing with the mobile phone. And, there are the X-box, the Kindle and the tablet or iPad. With the earphones plugged on, communication becomes almost impossible.

It is not much easier either, at times, to converse with older ones. The same gadgets and the free newspapers often get in the way, if the stiff upper lip does not get there first. Social media has replaced letter writing and most of the other forms of face-to-face conversation. And it is the latter that generates humour and laughter much more than the former.

There is also laughter inhibition. It has been estimated that children can laugh over 300 times a day. Adults, however, laughs less than 15 times a day. While there is usually a spontaneity about child laughter, an adult may suppress the urge to laugh, not wanting to 'look or sound childish'.

Mattheu Ricard, Budhist monk declared in 2008 the happiest man on earth, made the assertion that 15 minutes of laughter a day is needed for one to be described a 'happy' person. The next question that arises is: Are we less happy today than in the 1950s?

Researchers have come up with different answers to this question. BBC News Editor, Mark Easton, reported on the telephone poll carried out between 28th and 30th October 2005. The poll showed that in 1957, 52% of the population of the UK said that they were very happy, whereas, in 2005, only 37% of the population stated they were very happy. The editor also asserts that the British experience of this decline in happiness is mirrored by data from America, 'where social scientists have seen levels of life satisfaction decline over the last quarter of a century'.

TABLE 1.3 - BRITAIN'S HAPPINESS IN DECLINE (ADAPTED)

	1975	2006
Very Happy	52%	37%
Fairly Happy	41%	55%
Not Happy	6%	7%
Did Not Know	1%	1%

If we are getting less happy, why is that so? Some people blame technology. James Surowiecki, an American financial journalist and staff writer for the New Yorker stated: 'Technology is supposed to make our lives easier, allowing us to do things more quickly and efficiently. But too often, it seems to make things harder, leaving us with fifty-button remote controls, digital cameras with hundreds of mysterious features and book-length manuals and cars with dashboards systems worthy of the space shuttle.'

Professor Ed Diener of the University of Illinois, USA, stated: 'The idea that modern society is a sink of unhappiness seems wrong'. While it is clear that technology leads to a higher standard of living, better health care and longer life expectancy, it is not so clear if it is overall a blessing. Think of climate change. Worse still, think of the nuclear or hydrogen bomb. We have reached the moon and are poised to go further. Yet, we cannot solve numerous social problems on terra firma. On the opposite side of the argument is Professor F Halliwell of the University of British Columbia, Canada, who stated that happiness in the world is increasing. His 2012 World Health Report showed that out of the 125 countries surveyed, 53 countries experienced a significant increase in life satisfaction, an improvement over previous surveys.

MEASUREMENT OF PERSONAL HAPPINESS

Laughter happiness can be measured by using special sensors connected to the head. These can pick up gamma waves from the frontal cortex. Using this method, scientists at the University of Wisconsin, in 2008, declared Matthieu Ricard, a 66-year-old Tibetan monk, the happiest man on earth. Is the search for the happiest man on earth on-going?

READING LIST

1. Bremmer J (1997) Jokes, Jokers and Jokebooks in Ancient Greek Cultures. *In: J Bremmer and H Roodenburg, (Eds), A Cultural History of Humour* pp. 11 – 28. Malden, M A: Blackwell Publishers.

2. Panksepp J (2012) Laughter Across the Animal Kingdom, from Rats to Humans. Yale Scientific: November 4.

3. Shultz T R (1976) A Cognitive-Developmental Analysis of Humour. *In: A. J. Chapman and H. C. Foot (eds), Humour and Laughter: Theory, Research and Applications,* pp. 11 – 36. London: John Wiley and Sons.

4. Owren M J and Bachorowski J-A (2003) Reconsidering the Evolution of Non-linguistic Communication. *Journal of Non-verbal Behaviour,* 27(3) p. 187.

5. Provine R R L Laughter. *American Scientist,* vol 84, Jan/Feb 1996 p.40.

6. Freud S (1960) Jokes and their Relationship to the Unconscious. New York. W Norton, pp. 229 – 230

7. Veatch T C (1998) A Theory of Humour. *The International Journal of Humour Research,* May, 1998.

8. Jung W E (2003) The Inner Eye Theory of Laughter: Mind reader Signals Cooperator Value. *Evolutionary Psychology,* 1, 214 – 253.

9. Sherwin F (2004) The Origin of Laughter. *Acts and Facts;* 33-37.

10. McGraw A P and Warren C (2010) Benign Violation: Making Immoral Behaviour Funny. *Psychological Science,* 21, 1141 – 1149

11. The Evolution and Functions of Laughter and Humor: A Synthetic Approach. University of Chicago Press.

12. Mark E (2005) Britain's Happiness in Decline. British Broadcasting Corporation News Editor. BBC 2 broadcast, May 3.

13. Surowiecki J (2005). Technology and Happiness. *MIT Technology Review,* January.

14. World Health Report.(2013) Edited by John Halliwell, Richard Layard and Jeffrey Sachs Cambridge, MA: MIT Press. An edited book with chapters on various aspects of subjective well-being across nations.

15. Diener E and Suh E M (2000) Culture and Subjective Well-Being.

16. Rankin V and Attardo S (1991) Script Theory revisited: jokes similarity and joke representation model, In: Humour – *International Journal of Humour Research,* Volume 4, Issue 3 – 4, pp 293 – 348. Mouton de Grouper: Berlin, New York.

17. Zillman D and Bryant J (1985) Affect, Mood and Emotion As Determinants of Selective Exposure. *In: D Zillman and J Bryant (Eds.) Selective exposure to communication* pp 157 – 190. Hillside, NJ: Lawrence Erlbaum Associates.

18. Otto B K (2007) Fools Everywhere: The Court Jester Around the World. Chicago: University of Chicago Press.

CHAPTER 2
TYPES OF LAUGHTER

Laughter is classified mainly according to its intensity, the type of sound produced, its social context, the emotion that precipitates it and how it is perceived by others. Laughter types are, of course, not always mutually exclusive. Some types may have features that are common to others.

NB – Please feel free to try these types of laugh, having ensured privacy except you do not mind being thought of as loopy.

A] CLASSIFICATION OF LAUGHTER ACCORDING TO INTENSITY:

1. Smirk – This involves a slight and fleeting upturning of the corners of the mouth. No sound is produced.
2. Smile – Longer lasting upturning or the corners of the mouth. It is voluntary and controllable. Still, no sound is produced.
3. Grin – More facial muscles are used. For example, the eyes are partially closed. It is controllable. It is silent.
4. Snicker – It may last longer than a grin. Facial muscles may be involved. A small sound that is

difficult to control may be produced. Controlling a snicker leads to the building up of air in the lungs.

5. Giggle – A soft amusing sound is produced. An effort to suppress the sound increases the strength of the giggle and may start off giggling in those observing the giggler. Chest muscles are involved as air starts to build up in the lungs.
6. Chuckle – A deep-pitched sound is produced. Chest muscles are involved to a greater extent.
7. Chortle – Deep sounds are produced. Chest muscles are involved. Muscles of the torso are involved as well.
8. Cackle – High-pitched sounds are produced. Head may be turned upwards. The body may start to rock.
9. Guffaw – Loud deep sound is produced with arms waving and torso rocking. There may be feet stomping. Tears may flow. Breathlessness may ensue.
10. Roar – Loud raucous sounds are produced with loss of individuality or personality.
11. Convulsion – Low sounds are produced with a seizure. Extremities become flail. Balance may be lost. The subject may gasp for breath and fall. Even death may occur, though this is very rare.

B] CLASSIFICATION OF LAUGHTER BASED ON HOW IT IS PERCEIVED:

1. The Smile – The corners of the mouth are turned up slightly (as described in Classification A, above). A smile is silent, voluntary and completely controllable.

It is usually viewed positively by the person who is laughing and the beholder.

2. The Straight Ahead Laugh – This is a normal sounding laugh. Facial, thoracic and abdominal muscles are involved. It is more difficult to control.

3. The Grandfather Laugh - A deep continuous low-pitched noise is produced with the laugher holding the stomach.

4. The Guffaw - A deeper and louder noise than as in 3 above is produced. The muscles of the arms and are now involved. There may be the slapping of the thighs. It is very difficult to control this type of laughter.

5. The 'I laughed-so-hard I Could Have Cried' Laugh – Sounds as in 4 above are produced. The arms and feet are now kicking the air. The laugher may fall from standing or sitting and roll on the floor.

C] CLASSIFICATION OF LAUGHTER ACCORDING TO THE SOUND PRODUCED (ONOMATOPOEIA):

The basic sounds of laughter are ha, he or ho. The average duration of the ha, he or ho sound is 75 milliseconds while the average duration of the interval between the syllables is 210 milliseconds. The interval between syllables and groups of syllables and the way these sounds are grouped together during a laughter period form the basis for laughter classification as stated below.

1. HAHAHA LAUGHTER:

Hahaha, hehehe, hohoho – These are the syllables employed in laughter by people of all cultures. During this type of laughter, one does not attempt to catch one's breath between the syllables.

2. HA HA HA HA.....LAUGHTER:

Hahaha ha ha.... Hehehe he he he..... Hohoho ho ho ho... In this laughter pattern, the laughter is so long that the subject makes attempts to catch his or her breath at the end of a laughter period. He or she may then start to laugh all over again.

It is difficult to mix the laughter sounds stated above. Ha he ho or ho ho ha laughter does not exist. Also, it is worth mentioning that other laughter sounds such as, ke ke ke or ki ki ki and so on exist, but these occur less frequently. Also, gender, age and individuality exert some influence on laughter sound.

Another important characteristic of the laughter syllable ha, he or ho is the power (or pitch). This is a measure of the strength of the vibrations or frequency produced in the vocal chords. It is measured in hertz. The average frequency for natural laughter is 270 hertz for a man and 220 hertz for a female. This frequency can go up to 1500 hertz during a forced laughter, such as a guffaw. Females can reach even higher frequencies. Please note that the average frequency for ordinary speech is 120 hertz.

Various combinations or variations of the basic patterns above are described in Table 2.1 below.

TABLE 2.1 - LAUGHTER SOUND PATTERNS

Pattern	Description
Hahaa, hehehe, hohoho	Basic
Hahaha ha ha ha…, hehehe he he he… and hohoho ho ….	Long spells of laughter with an attempt to catch one's breath.
Kekekekeke	Childish laughter with the mouth covered with the hand.
Har har har har	Laughter with sarcastic intent.
HO HO HO HO HO	Laughter with Santa 'Claus' jollity.
MWAHAHAHAHA………	Laugher with an evil intent.

OTHER TYPES OF LAUGHTER ARE:

Voiced and unvoiced laughter - Voiced laughter is, obviously, produced from the vocal cords. It is tonal and spontaneous, resulting in the sound of vowel-like quality. Belly laugh is an example.

Unvoiced laughter, however, consists of pants, grunts or snorts. This type of laughter is more than a smile but is less than a belly laugh. It is produced as a result of air turbulence in the laryngeal and nasal cavities.

Dr William Hudenko, a psychologist at Ithaca College, made some observations about voiced and unvoiced types of laughter:

1. Voiced and unvoiced types of laughter originate from different parts of the brain. Voiced laughter is controlled in the part of the brain called the neocortex, while unvoiced laughter is controlled in the part, called the paleocortex or old brain. These terms denote the time on the evolutionary scale that these areas developed morphologically.
2. According to Hudenko, male laughter contains more unvoiced than the voiced variety. Female laughter is more of the voiced type.
3. Voiced laughter is used mainly to negotiate social interactions while unvoiced laughter is used to express internalised happiness.
4. Autistic children have limited ability to produce voiced laughter.

'We need more research to understand better the nature and function of voiced versus unvoiced laughter', Dr Hudenko concludes.

Duchene laughter - According to Dr Guillaume Duchenne, a French neurologist, who first described it, this type of laughter is voluntary and authentic or genuine in contrast to forced or faked laughter. It involves the zygomatic major muscle which raises the corners of the mouth and the cheeks with 'crow's feet' forming in the lateral corners of the eyes and the orbicularis oculi muscles which partially close the eyes.

Duchene laughter is usually associated with positive emotions.

Fake laughter- At urbandictionary.com, synonyms used for fake laughter include false laughter, lie laughter, pretend laughter and conned laughter. Then this definition is provided: 'an outburst of laughter done to act as if something was found funny but in reality it wasn't'. The dictionary then states that fake laughter can be annoying and it can diminish the status of the fake laugher before the person who makes the joke.

An example of a faked laughter is when the boss tells a joke that is regarded as not funny and the subordinates laugh anyway. The fake laugher knows, of course, that his or her laughter is fake. How about the joker? Can we tell when a laugh is fake?

Greg Bryant, Assistant Professor of Communication Studies at UCLA and his associates conducted studies from which they concluded that acoustics and breath qualities differ between fake and genuine laughter. When fake laughter is speeded up, the participants in the study found that it sounded more genuine. More significantly, they found that fake laughter was recognised by observers for what it is, fake, about 66% of the time. In other words, laughter can be faked about one-third of the time. 'That is a rather high success rate', some might say.

Dr Carolyn McGettigen of the Department of Psychology, University of London, studied the reaction of people who listened to recordings of fake and genuine laughter. Measurements of neurological reactions to the different types of laughter were found to have come from different regions of the brain. She concluded that fake laughter is controlled by the area of the brain that controls emotions, while, genuine laughter is controlled by region that controls happiness. This agrees with the claim by neuroscientists, that, genuine laughter is primitive, whereas, fake laughter is unique to humans.

Canned laughter – Canned laughter is live audience laughter that is recorded and played later during a comedy show. It is a type of fake laughter.

Canned laughter was created in the early 1960s by 'Charley' Douglas, an American sound engineer. Notable comedy shows that used or still use canned laughter include: Friends (in the USA) and Mr.Bean (in the UK).

The reason for using canned laughter is that it provokes laughter in an at-home audience. It exploits the contagious effects of laughter, which can be mostly enjoyable. However, the opposite effect may ensue. Some people may find canned laughter annoying if they feel that the comic performance is not funny after all.

Nervous laughter – This type of laughter is evoked, not by amusement, but by an individual's embarrassment, discomfort or confusion. It is produced in the throat. It is usually not as intense as belly laugh. Neuroscientists, Robert Provine (cited earlier) and neuro-scientists V. S. Ramachandran, consider nervous laughter as a means of relieving tension or anxiety.

Nervous laughter is also referred to as a courtesy laughter. This occurs, for an example, when a joker pauses, waiting for a laugh from the audience.

Nervous laughter is a form of fake laughter. Rather than relieving tension, it can intensify it. It can also become a habit that is difficult to overcome.

Pathological or paradoxical laughter – Is an exaggerated type of laughter. It is uncontrollable, unwarranted and is not commensurate with the stimulus producing it. Observers often regard this type of laughter inappropriate.

At times, laughter changes abruptly into crying. This phenomenon is associated with altered mental states such as: mania, hypo-mania and schizophrenia. Pathological conditions that can lead to laughter changing into crying includes - brain tumours, strokes, multiple sclerosis, epilepsy and pseudo-bulbar palsy.

Electronic or e-laughter – This is the way we 'laugh' and encourage others to 'laugh' with us on the internet. At the end of a joke or some funny statement, we can convey our hilarity and our invitation for the recipient to join in with us by using expressions like hahaha, ho ho ho, hehehe or various combinations of these laughter syllables. At times, the abbreviation, LOL, may be used. This does not mean Lots of Love. What is funny about that? It is inviting the recipient of our message to Laugh Out Loud.

A recent development is the use of Emojis. This term stands for electronic images. At Dictionary.com, an emoji is defined as: 'a small digital picture or pictorial symbol that represents a thing, feeling, concept etc., used in text messages and other electronic communication and usually part of a standardised set'. The Oxford English Dictionary puts it more succinctly: 'An emoji is a digital image or icon used to express an idea or emotion in electronic communication'.

The term emoji is of Japanese origin. E, of course, stands for Electronic. Moji is the Japanese word for a letter, character or icon.

Emojis are now all over our mobile phones, especially the smartphones. It was the brainchild of Shigeteka Kurita, an employee of the Japanese telecommunication company, NTT Docomo. In the early 1990s, he developed the idea of adding cartoon images to the company's messaging functions as a way to appeal to teenagers. Kurita designed about 176 icons. Today, more than 722 Emojis exist.

LAUGHTER AND INDIVIDUALITY:

Do laughter sounds vary between individuals? Matt Petronzio, an American poet, and journalist based in New York, thinks so. In his description of the geography of laughter, he refers to the uniqueness of laughter sounds uttered by individuals – Eddy Murphy's breathless guffaw, Nick Offerman's unexpected giggle and Fran Drescher's nasally titter.

Differences in laughter sounds produced by individuals are mediated by variations in anatomy, psychology and human behaviour. However, these variations are not significant. Provine agrees. 'Laughter should not be treated as speech,' he asserts. 'Laughter, like crying, has more in common with the barking of a dog.'

The only authentic laughter is the spontaneous one. This is the type of laughter displayed when we are on our own. It varies little between individuals.

LAUGHTER AND CULTURE/ETHNICITY*

Do people of different ethnic or cultural groups laugh differently? This question is not about what makes people of different cultures laugh. Rather, it is about the laughter sounds made by people belonging to different ethnic backgrounds. If we listened to but do not see people laughing, will we be able to identify the cultural group they belong to?

Jennifer Warner, a freelance writer and educator based in Minneapolis, Minnesota, USA, reported on a study led by Professor Sophie Scott, a neuroscientist and stand-up comic. In the study, participants from the UK and the Himba tribe of northern Namibia listened to each other's laughter sounds. The conclusion from the study is that laughter sounds are easier to recognise than other sounds made in response to other emotions such as sadness, anger, or embarrassment.

However, some researchers claim that people hailing from different cultures laugh differently. Dr Moira Smith of the University of Indiana, reported on a study of 3 cultural groups – the Bushmen of southern Africa, Tamils of South India and Samoans living in Auckland, New Zealand.

No major difference was found in the quality of the laughter sounds produced by the Bushmen in the study. Rather, the subjects displayed unique personal behaviour. They were found to hold each other and slap their thighs.

Tamils in the study laughed with a distinctive feature - the rhythm of the laughter sounds. This was found to be slower and more evenly spaced than that for the other cultural groups. The laughter sounds of the Samoans were found to be more high-pitched and falsetto than those of other groups. These observations show that there are slight differences in laughter sounds (onomatopoeia) produced by different cultural groups.

TABLE 2.2 - DIFFERENT LAUGHTER SOUNDS PRODUCED BY SOME ETHNIC GROUPS

Group	Laughter Sound
Arabic	Ha ha ha; he he he
Chinese (Mandarin)	Ha ha; he he
English	Hahah hah hah
French	Ha ha ha; he he he; hi hi hi; hon hon hon
German	Ha ha ha; hi hi hi
Italian	Ah ah ah; eh eh eh; hi hi hi; uh uh uh
Japanese	Aha ha ha
Russian	Ha ha; xa xa; hi hi
Spanish	Ja ja ja; je je je

NB: Definitions of culture, ethnicity and race.

Culture - A particular society that has its own set of beliefs, a way of life, norms that unite it.

Ethnicity – People belonging to a socially defined category who identify with one another based on common social, cultural experiences, language, religion, custom, geographical location.

Race – People with similar genetic origin, hence similar morphology. Unlike ethnicity, race is not subject to choice.

READING LIST

1. Bachorowski J A, Smoski M J and Owren M J (2001) The Acoustic Features of Human Laughter. *The Journal of the Acoustical Society of America,* 110(1): 1581 – 1597
2. Bachorowski J A and Owren M J (2001) Not All Laughters Are Alike; Vocal But Not Unvoiced Laughter. *Science,* 12: 252 – 257.
3. Smoski M J and Barochowski J A (2003) Anti-phonal Laughter Between Friends and Strangers. *Cognition and Emotion,* 17: 327 – 340.
4. Owren M J anS Barochowski J A (2003) Sounds of Emotion. *Annals of the New York Academy of sciences,* 1000(1): 244 – 265.
5. Hudenko WJ, Stone 2 and Barochowski J A (2009) Laughter Differs In Children With And Without Autism: An Analysis of Laughs Produced By hildren With And Without the Disorder. *Journal of Autism And Developmental Disorders,* 39(1-): 1392 – 1400.
6. Provine R R (1991) Laughter: A Stereotype Human Vocalization. *Ethology;* 89: 115 – 124.
7. Provine R R (1993) Laughter Punctuates Speech: Linguistic and Gender Contexts of Laughter. *Ethology;* 95; 291 - 298.
8. Wildgruber D, Szamallat D P Ethofer T, Bruck K A, Grodd W, Krefelts B (2013) Differerent Types of Laughter Modulate Connectivity Within Part of the Laughter Perception Network. Public Library of Science.

CHAPTER 3
THE BASIC ANATOMY OF LAUGHTER

The production of laughter is due to muscles around the face, throat and chest. These muscles give the expression of mirth to the face, force air from the lungs to passout of or into the lungs and fine-tune the flow of air through the epiglottis to produce laughter sounds.

Please see Table 3.1 for the list of the facial muscles that are involved in the production of laughter.

The muscles named in Table 3.1 plus muscles in the neck, back, arms and legs come into action for the production of belly laugh and the 'I-laughed-till-I-nearly-died' type of laughter.

Please note that the names of the muscles listed (like all names of muscles) are rather descriptive. Knowledge of Latin does facilitate the understanding of the meaning of the names. If you do not have that knowledge, just try to understand the actions performed by the muscles. This will help you to understand the muscles' actions.

TABLE 3.1 - FACIAL MUSCLES AND THEIR ACTIONS

	Muscle	Origin	Insertion	Action
1	Zygomaticus	Zygomatic	The skin	Draws the

	major) x2	arch (cheekbone)	over the angle of the mouth	angle of the mouth upwards and backwards
2	Zygomaticus minor x2	As above	As above	Draws the angle of the mouth upwards and backwards
3	Orbicularis oris x1	Its fibres originate from the upper jaw and from other muscles that surround the mouth	Its fibres encircle the mouth and are inserted into other the skin and other muscles that surround the mouth	This muscle closes or purses the lips
4	Orbicularis oculi x2	Its fibres encircle the eyes	The fibres are inserted into the eye lids	It closes the eye lids and compresses the tear

				gland to bring about the flow of tears over the eyes.
5	Risorius x2	The cheek	The skin over the angle of the mouth	Draws the angle of the mouth outwards
6	Elevator labii superioris x2	The bone in the upper part of the eye socket	The skin of the upper lip	It draws the angle of the mouth upwards and backwards
7	Levator anguli oris x2	The bone in the lower part of the eye socket.	The skin over the angle of the mouth	
8	Platysma x1	The lower jaw	The fascia under the skin over the chin, front of the neck and	It draws the lower lip down

			spreading over the neck down the front part of the chest to the level of the 2nd rib	
9	Mentalis x1	The skin between the chin and the lips	The skin between the chin and the lips	It wrinkles the skin over the chin. It also elevates and protrudes the lower lip
10	Corrugator supercilii x2	The cartilage in the root of the nose	The skin of the eye brows	
11	Procerus x1	The skin over the bridge of the nose	The skin between the eye brows	It wrinkles the skin over the nose
12	Depressor anguli oris x2	The skin over the medial	The skin of the	It pulls the angle of the mouth

		angle of the eye	eye brow	downwards
13	Nasalis x1	The maxilla or upper jaw	Nasal cartilages	It pulls the lips upwards and dilates the nostrils
14	Buccinator x1	The maxilla and mandible (upper and lower jaws)	The skin over the angle of the mouth	It keeps the cheeks against the teeth and retracts the angle of the mouth
15	Frontalis x1	This muscle is situated in the forehead. It is part of the much larger flat muscle, the occipito-frontalis that arises from the fascia that covers the scalp	The skin over the forehead	It furrows the skin over the forehead and raises the eyebrow.

TABLE 3.2 - SOME ACTIVITIES AND THE MUSCLES THAT PRODUCE THEM

Action	Muscle involved
Smiling	Levator anguli
Normal laughter	Zygomaticus
Grinning	Risorius
Sadness or grief	Depressor anguli oris
Doubt	Mentalis
Discontent	Levator labii superioris alaque nasi
Menace	Procerus
Satisfaction	Buccinator
Surprise or astonishment	Frontalis
Reserve	Orbicularis oris
Concern	Orbicularis oculi

A frequently asked question is: How many muscles are involved in the production of laughter? A common answer is: It takes 43 muscles to frown and 17 to laugh. This is often followed by the advice to laugh more as if it is less strenuous to do so than to frown. (See Appendix 10 for a variety of answers to the question. Some of the answers are quite fallacious.)

This is patently false. According to Dr David Song, a plastic surgeon and an Associate Professor at Chicago

University Hospitals (he should know), 12 muscles are involved in the production of a smile, 11 for producing a frown and more than forty can be recruited to produce laughter. It all depends on the intensity of the laughter produced. So, the world of laughter is not necessarily a lazy one.

TABLE 3.3 - SOME FALLACIOUS STATEMENTS ABOUT HOW MANY MUSCLES INVOLVED IN PRODUCING A SMILE OR A FROWN.

Statement	Source
It takes 13 muscles to smile and 33 to frown. Why overwork?	The Washington Post, December 5, 1982.
We use only 4 muscles to smile but when we frown we use 64 muscles.	The Hindu, March 11, 2000.
It only takes 10 muscles to smile but it takes 100 to frown.	A lady quoted in The New York Times, April 19, 1987.
It takes 4 muscles to smile, 20 to frown and roughly 317 to appear to be amused.	The Denver Post, September 29, 1998.
It is easier to smile than to frown. A smile uses 17 muscles, a frown 43.	Milwaukee Journal Sentinel, February 24, 1977.
It only takes 1 muscle to smile, 37 to frown.	St Louis Post-Dispatch, April 24, 1995.

It takes 72 muscles to frown – only 14 to smile.	Encyclopaedia of 7700 Illustrations, 1979.
It takes 15 muscles to smile and 65 to frown. This leads me to believe that X is suffering from muscle fatigue	The New York Times, December 16, 1986.

THE NEUROLOGY OF LAUGHTER:

The human brain is extremely complex. As intimated earlier, a detailed consideration of the brain's anatomy and physiology is outside the scope of this book. What follows is a basic account of how the brain controls laughter.

Figures 1, 2 and 3 show the basic shape and inner structure of the human brain.

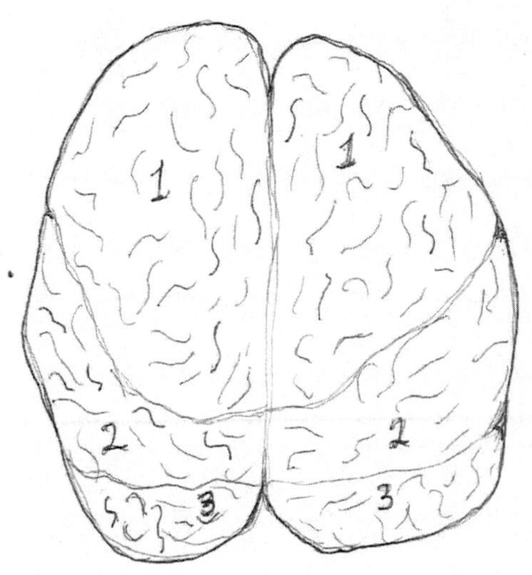

Figure 1 – Top View of the Human Brain

FIG. 4.2 THE BRAIN – LEFT SIDE VIEW

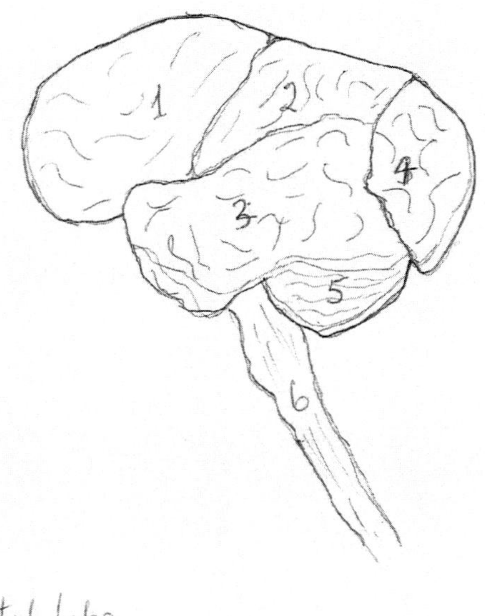

KEY:

1 – Frontal lobe
2 – Parietal lobe
3 – Temporal lobe
4 – Occipital lobe
5 – Cerebellum
6 – Brain stem

Figure 2 – Side View of the Human Brain

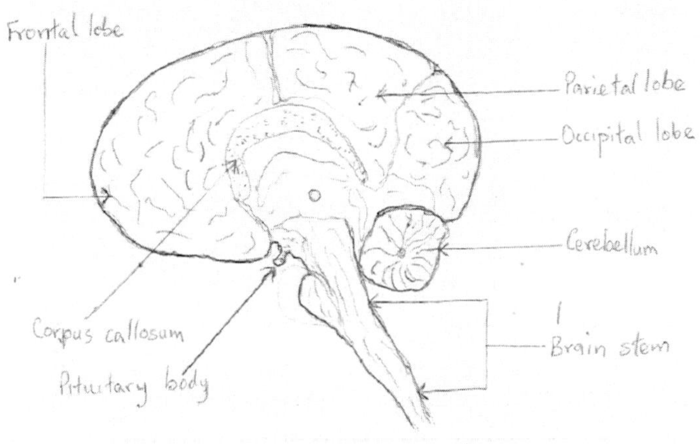

Figure 3 – Median View of the Human Brain

The scientific study of how the brain controls humour and laughter started in the 19th century AD. It was mainly abnormal laughter (resulting from brain pathology) that was studied. For an example, post-mortem examination of the brain was used to determine which area of the brain was affected leading to abnormal laughter.

More recently, a start has been made in studying how the brain controls normal laughter. The method of Electroencephalography (EEG), Magnetic Resonance Imaging (MRI) and Positron Emission Tomography (PET) scanning have been started to be used to find out which areas of the brain are active during various types of laughter.

Scientists believe that laughter is controlled by complicated circuitries in the brain. According to these scientists, a complex web of neurones connect the centres in the different part of the brain. The circuitries can be grouped into three parts: the parts that control emotion, the parts that control cognition and those that control laughter muscles.

Please see Table 3.4

TABLE 3.4 - THE BASIC FORMAT OF THE BRAIN'S CONTROL OF LAUGHTER

Part of the Brain	Function
Left lobe	Analysis of words and structure of the 'joke' stimuli.
Right lobe	Intellectual analysis of 'joke' stimuli. This is required for the person to 'get the joke'.
Occipital lobe	Further analysis of the 'joke'.
Motor areas of Left and Right lobes	Production of physical (muscular) response to the 'joke'.

Strong joke stimuli will produce stronger laughter reaction. The stimuli penetrate deeper into the brain and reach the area collectively called the Limbic System. Please see Table 4.2 for a basic breakdown of the functions of the various neural bodies that make up the Limbic System. These parts are connected to themselves and other parts of the brain by complicated circuitries that mediate and modify laughter.

The Limbic System consists of 4 major parts with these tongue-twisting names – the Amygdala, the Thalamus, the Hypothalamus and the Hippocampus. Please see Figure 4 for the basic anatomy of the Limbic System

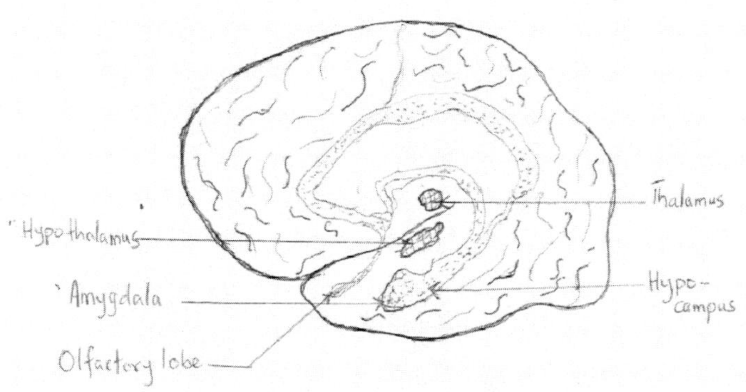

Figure 4 – The Limbic System

Table 3.5 overleaf shows the functions of the main parts of the Limbic System.

TABLE 3.5 - THE FUNCTIONS OF PARTS OF THE LIMBIC SYSTEM

Part	Function
Amygdala	Controls activities like friendship, love, affection and other moods.
Thalamus	Regulates body temperature and the consistency of the cells' internal environment.
Hypothalamus	Controls the production of loud uncontrollable laughter.
Hippocampus	Plays a major role in short-term and long-term memory and spatial navigation.

There are two main factors that affect the brain's perception of humour and the subsequent laughter response. These are - age and gender.

AGE AND LAUGHTER:

Children laugh at short and simple concepts and events taking place around them. Preteens tend to be generally awkward, while teens relish poking fun and laughing at what adults consider off-limits. Teens, use laughter as a tool for protection and to feel superior. Humour or laughter by adults is characterised by increased subtlety and tolerance. Adults, having experienced predicaments and embarrassments, display a higher degree of wit or intelligence needed to 'get the joke'.

LAUGHTER AND GENDER:

Dr Moira Smith of Indiana University conducted a study of 1200 adults. In her study she found that showed women laughed 126% more than men.

Though women tend to laugh more often than men, women do not laugh as intensely as men. Belly laugh is not described as grand-father laugh for nothing. Also, men do more of laugh getting than women who do more of laughing. It is men who initiate humour generally.

Men are regarded by some writers as funnier than women. Make what you like of that. What evolutionary psychologists make of it is that sense of humour is genetic. The humour gene endows men with wit and intellect, qualities that make them attractive to women. Women seek to have these genes bestowed upon their offspring.

Kim Edwards of the University of Western Ontario, Canada, contradicts this view. In 2005, he conducted a study from which he concluded: 'the greater laughter garnered by men is more a consequence of social factors than a sign of a superior capacity for humour production'. To him/her, sense of humour is nurture, not nature.

Scott Barry Kaufman of New York University describes sense of humour in terms of sexual selection. He explains: "When you have little else to go on, a witty person who uses humour in a clever way is signalling quite a lot of information including intelligence creativity and even aspects of their personality such as playfulness and openness to experiment".

Please see Table 3.6 below. It lists some assertions by Provine (cited earlier) that seem to strengthen the view that males do more than females in generating humour or laughter. Conversely, females do more of the laughing.

TABLE 3.6 - GENDER RESPONSE TO LAUGHER (ADAPTED FROM PROVINE [2005])

Speaker	Audience	Type of response
Male	Female	Speaker laughs 7% less than the audience
Female	Male	Speaker laughs 127% more than the audience.

Male	Mixed	Audience laughs more than speaker.
Female	Mixed	Audience laughs least*

The lot of the comedienne is not an easy one.

Also, please see Appendix 4.

LAUGHTER CONTAGION:

The 1962 laughter epidemic in Tanganyika (now Tanzania) is often referred to when the contagious nature of laughter is discussed. Three pupils, in a school in Kashasha on the shore of Lake Tanganyika and close to the Ugandan border, started to laugh. The laughing spread to other pupils in the school and led to the closure of the school. The laughter then spread to other schools in other areas and persisted for six to eighteen months, depending on who is recounting the event. Fourteen schools and about one thousand pupils were said to have been affected.

One major observation about the event is that those affected were mostly young school girls and not their teachers or older members of the communities. It is agreed by examiners of the event that something peculiar happened at the time. However, it was not about humour or real laughter. It is now known that laughter was only a part of it. Other parts were crying, pain, flatulence, rashes, fainting respiratory problems and random screaming. The term used for the condition is Mass Psychogenic Illness (MPI) or Mass Hysteria.

A more recent and easier-to-explain example of contagious laughter is the 1991 comment by Jonathan Agnew, British Broadcasting Corporation cricket commentator. England was playing against the West Indies at the Oval in the last match of the Test series. The legendary cricketer, Sir Ian Botham, hit his own wicket. Aggers, as the reporter is affectionately known, stated that the batsman was out because he failed to get his leg clear of the wicket as he fell backwards. Agnew started to giggle and laugh in paroxysms and infected his co-commentator, the late Brian Johnston, and others in the commentary box. They all giggled and laughed uncontrollably, infecting thousands who listened later to their laughter on the radio and on television.

READING LIST

1. Provine R R (2000) Laughter: A Scientific Investigation. Penguin Books, New York, NY. Page 650.
2. Tierney J (2013) What's Funny? Well, Maybe Nothing. Reported in The New York Times of March 13, 2013.
3. Beard M (2008) Isn't It Funny? New York Review of Books (June 2011).
4. Azim E (2005) Sex Differences in Brain Activation Elicited by Humor. *Proceedings of the National Academy of Sciences in the United States of America,* 102(45), 16496 – 16501
5. Berns G (2004) Something Funny Happened to Reward. *Trends in Cognitive Sciences,* 8(5) 193 – 194.
6. Wild B (2003) Neural Co-relates of laughter and humour. *Brain,* 126(10), 2121 – 2138.
7. Walker R (2003) The Lives They Lived: Making Us Laugh. The New York Times, June 1, 2009.

8. Longstaff B (2001) Girls Giggle and Guys Grunt. New Scientist Article; September 27.
9. Sebastian S (2003) Examining 1962's laughter epidemic. Chicago Tribune, July 29.

CHAPTER 4
THE BENEFITS OF LAUGHTER

The notion that laughter is good for health is a very old one. Some 3000 years ago, Wise King Solomon wrote: "A cheerful heart is good medicine but a broken spirit makes you sick" - Proverbs chapter 17 verse 22. See Appendix 2 for alternative renderings of this saying.

To many people, laughter is not just good medicine. It is "the best medicine". It has been credited with positive effects that include the alleviation of pain, boosting of immunity, prevention of heart disease and the reduction of weight. Some researchers assert that laughter is a powerful tool in the treatment of cancer. Psycho-social benefits attributed to laughter include: the relief of stress and anxiety, improvement in memory and creativity and the ability to make friends and influence people.

Please see Table 4.1 below for the generic benefits of laughter.

TABLE 4.1 - GENERIC BENEFITS OF LAUGHTER

Health Benefits	Mental benefits	Social Benefits
Decrease in Pain	Improvement of Mood	Promotion of bonding
Lowering of Physical Stress	Decrease of Mental Stress	Enhancement of teamwork
Boost of Immunity	Increase of zest and joy of life	Resolution of conflict
Muscle Relaxation	Improvement in memory	Increase in inter-personal attraction
Increase in Blood Circulation		

These quotes below are from the *Watching the World* series in the journal Awake published by the Watch Tower Bible and Tract Society. They provide enthusiastic support for laughter as a curer

1. Awake, October 22, 2005 – 'Scientists have calculated that only half a minute of joyful laughter is worth 45 minutes of static rest,' reports the Polish weekly PRZYJACIOLKA. 'A spontaneous burst of laughter is comparable to 3 minutes of aerobic exercise whereas 10 warm smiles equal 10 of intensive rowing.' Other benefits of laughing include a three-fold increase in the amount of air drawn into the lungs as well as improved circulation, digestion, metabolism, brain function and elimination of harmful substances. The

magazine suggests that to help put yourself in the right mood, you should smile at yourself, your mate and your children first thing in the morning. 'Learn to laugh at yourself' it adds. 'Try to find good side of things even in difficult circumstances.'

2. Awake, December 22, 2004 – 'Neurologists at Stamford University have discovered another reason why laughter makes us feel good,' reports the UC Berkley WELLNESS LETTER. 'They monitored the brain activity of people reading funny cartoons and found that humour or laughter triggered the brain's "reward centers", the same areas affected by stimulant drugs. 'Laughter reduces tension, clears the mind, and lifts the spirit,' says the Wellness Letter. Laughter also increases our hormone production and heart rate, and it contributes to better circulation and muscle tone. Indeed, a good laugh is a kind of workout,' notes the Wellness Letter. 'It is not exactly a major calorie burner, however. You can laugh yourself silly but not thin.'

3. Awake, March 8, 2002 – 'A dose of comedy taken daily for 4 weeks has now been found to reduce significantly the symptoms of depression,' reports The Independent of London. 'Some of the patients who were told to spend 30 minutes a day listening to therapeutic tapes of comedians were cured while others found that the severity of their symptoms had been halved.' More than 100 studies in the United States have indicated that laughter induced by humour can be beneficial. Not only to people who are depressed but also to those who had allergies, high blood pressure, weakened immune systems and even

cancer and rheumatism have responded. Laughter has long been known to promote well-being, but how is not clearly understood. Psychotherapist Dr Ed Dumkleblau, offers some cautionary advice, though. Avoid abusive and sarcastic humour and be careful about being too funny. Otherwise, the patient may feel that his problem is not being taken seriously.

4. Awake, December 8, 2002 – Good-natured laughter does more than brighten a person's day. According to some Japanese doctors, it also normalises imbalances in the endocrine, nervous, and immune, stabilises heart beat ad breathing, and can bring temporary relief to sufferers of rheumatism. Laughter stimulates sympathetic nerves thereby boosting the blood flow to muscles and brain activity. When we laugh heartily, we also our muscles. In a test cited in the IHT Asahi Shimbun newspaper, one laughing subject's abdominal muscles 'showed the same level of exertion as required by sit-ups.' Osaka based psychologist Michio Tanaka praised the use positive influence of laughter. According to Tanaka, 'it is like an effective drug with no side effects.'

5. Awake, February 22, 1997 – It has long been believed that laughter is good medicine. Ten years ago scientists at the State University of New York decided to find out why that is. They recently revealed their discovery that laughter helps trigger the release of powerful hormones that energises a person's immune system. One group of hormones called cytokines has been found to promote the activity of white blood cells which are needed to ward off viral and bacterial infections and which destroy cancer cells. These are

just 'one of the substances whose levels are increased by laughter', says The Sunday Times of London. The link between laughter and cytokines has led some researchers to refer to them as happy hormones. Thus, the paper calls laughter 'a recipe for a long life'.

Tests reveal that sustained laughter can reduce pain as well as be a good workout for the heart. Circulation improves, the diaphragm is exercised and the oxygen level in the blood is raised. Chest, neck, face and scalp muscles also get a workout along with eye muscles that expel tears.

The Journal of the American Medical Association reported on a study that 'suggests that a humour therapy programme can increase the quality of life of the patients with chronic problems and that laughter has an immediate symptom-relieving effect for these patients'.

The result of the psychological approach to rehabilitation prompted the British Columbia Cancer agency to add a humour room to their library.

Simply laughing our way through life, however, will not ensure good health. Rather,a balance is needed. The Bible says that there is a time to laugh and a time to be quiet. Thoughtless laughter may grate on the ears of others and is compared to the sound of crackling thorns being burned under a pot because it is useless and offers no edification – Ecclesiastes 3 verse 4 and 7 verse 6.

The claims cited above are more anecdotal than scientific. Those provided below are claims that have more scientific backing. They are reports of randomised controlled studies.

1. THE EFFECT OF LAUGHTER ON PAIN

Some researchers claim that the most prominent benefit of laughter is the reduction of pain. Norman Cousins, an American journalist and author, claimed that 10 minutes of laughter had up to two hours of analgesic effect on the pain he suffered from ankylosing spondylitis, a rheumatic condition that affects the spine.

Dr Robin Dunbar, an anthropologist and experimental psychologist at Oxford University, England, reported on a study that he and his colleagues conducted on the effects of laughter. The subjects of the study were members of the Oxford University rowing team. Pain threshold was measured before and after the participants had watched humorous TV clips of Mr Bean and/or Friends. Also, measurement of pain threshold was done with the participants on their own and in groups. The conclusions from the study were:

a) 'When laughter is elicited, pain thresholds are significantly increased whereas when subjects watched something that does not normally elicit laughter, pain thresholds do change.'

b) 'Watching about 15 minutes of comedy in a group increases pain threshold by 10%.'

How does laughter bring pain relief? Two explanations are offered.

The first is that laughter excites the frontal lobes. Pain-reducing enzymes, endorphin and encephalin are produced in these areas of the brain. Exercise, emotional excitement, sexual arousal and orgasm, eating spicy food and smoking cannabis and or other opioid substances affect this area of the brain. These activities, like laughter, raise the pain threshold.

The second is that laughter brings about relaxation of muscles by decreasing the amount of pain-producing substances that accompany muscle tension and fatigue.

2. THE EFFECT OF LAUGHTER ON INFECTION AND IMMUNITY:

Researchers claim that laughter can help to fight existing infections and provide the subject with the ability to fight future infections.

According to Dr Lee Berk and Dr Stanley Tan of Loma Linda University, California, USA, belly laughter can increase a person's white blood cells count. They assert that 1 hour of laughing when viewing a funny video can produce a 24-hour increase in the number of white blood cells. A study by Dr Mary Bennett of Western Kentucky University School of Nursing, found that 33 healthy women who laughed watching a humorous movie experienced a rise in the level of T-cells and non-killer cells in their blood. T-cells are a type of white blood cells called lymphocytes. Their role is to "hunt down and destroy cells that are infected by germs (or bacteria)". Non-killer cells are a special type of T-cells. Their role is to "orchestrate" an immune response to infection. How does laughter increase the ability to fight infection and raise immunity? Neuro-scientists state that the brain and the organs that produce chemicals that fight infection, the thymus and bone marrow, are 'wired together'. The structures have receptors that can receive laughter-mediated impulses originating from the frontal lobe of the brain. Laughter appears to turn on the systems for fighting and preventing infections.

Dr Dunbar asserts that there is a strong link between laughter and immunity. He emphasises that the lymphatic system is the backbone of the immune system.

The blood circulatory system has a pump, the heart. This is in sharp contrast, to the lymphatic system. It needs pressure in the thoracic cavity to move lymph up the thoracic lymphatic duct. According to Dr Robin Dunbar (cited earlier) and his colleagues, belly laugh provides this pressure. They maintain that the negative pressure created by movement of the diaphragm during strenuous laughter can move lymph through the thoracic duct at up to fifteen times the normal rate. The increased flow of lymphatic fluid means increased passage of lymphocytes through the lymph nodes into the blood. This increase results in increase in the number of killer cells that fight infection and promote immunity.

3. THE EFFECT OF LAUGHTER ON STRESS

The same study mentioned above by Dr Lee Berk showed that subjects who laughed experienced a decrease in the amount of the stress hormones, cortisol, epinephrine and dopamine in their blood in contrast to subjects who did not laugh.

Dr Mary Bennett and others at the Indiana State University Sycamore Nursing Centre conducted a randomised study of the effect of laughter on stress. The subjects were 33 healthy women. One group of the subjects watched a funny video, while the control group watched a distraction video about tourism. Self-Reported Stress Arousal Checklist and Humour Response Scale were used to measure each group's pre and post video watching stress levels. The overall stress level for the group that watched a funny video was found to be significantly lower than for the group that watched the tourism video.

Also, researchers at California's Loma Linda University conducted a study with a group of about twenty men and women aged between 60 to 70 years. The subjects were then divided into two groups. While one group sat silently and read or used their cell phones for twenty minutes, the other group watched funny videos also for twenty minutes. The researchers used the amount of the hormone cortisol present in the subjects' saliva to assess their pre and post-test levels of stress.

How does laughter bring about a lowering of stress? Cortisol is the chemical substance that increases stress. Laughter is known to lead to a decrease in the amount of this hormone in the blood and thus, laughter can relieve stress.

4. THE EFFECT OF LAUGHTER ON BLOOD PRESSURE

Dr Madan Kataria, the founder of Laughter Yoga, conducted, with other researchers, a study into the effect of laughter on blood pressure. One hundred subjects took part in fake laughter for 45 seconds in every minute for about 20 minutes. Breathing exercises and stretching were also practised. Seven sessions were undertaken over three weeks. It was found that at the end of the 'treatment' session, the subjects experienced a significant reduction in both systolic and diastolic blood pressure compared to 100 other subjects who did not take part in the Yoga laughter.

TABLE 4.2 - CHANGES IN THE BLOOD PRESSURE AFTER 3 WEEKS OF LAUGHTER YOGA (ADAPTED FROM KATARIA ET AL).

Measurement	Laughter Yoga Group (n=200)	Control Group (n=100)
Pre-treatment systolic blood pressure (mm Hg)	128.24	125.89
Post-treatment blood systolic pressure 9mm Hg)	120.78	125.99
Change (in %)	-6.18	+0.06
Pre-treatment systolic blood pressure	82.37	82.34
Post-treatment systolic	79.34	81.8

blood pressure		
Change (in %)	-3.82	-0.65

Commenting on the result of this study, Dr Kataria said that 'extended laughter' of the belly laugh type is needed to bring about physiological and biochemical changes. Real life laughter, he argued, is too short in duration to exert significant health benefits.

How does laughter bring about a reduction in blood pressure? There is a strong correlation between stress and blood pressure. The same hormone, cortisol, controls both. Cortisol produces the 'fight or flight' response. As the blood vessels constrict, blood pressure rises. Laughter has the effect of reducing the secretion of cortisol and thus, reduces vasoconstriction which in turn leads to a reduction in blood pressure.

5. THE EFFECT OF LAUGHTER ON DEPRESSION

Dr Nasr J Subayl, Professor of Psychiatry, Indiana University, reported on a single case study. A 56-year-old lady with bipolar depression survived several suicide attempts and did not respond to mood stabilisers and ECT. After she participated in Laughter Therapy for several months, (the exact length of the period of participation was not stated), her mood stabilised and she eventually became a Laughter Yoga instructor.

Dr H J Ko of the College of Pharmacy, Dankook University, Cheonan, Republic of Korea and Dr C H Youn, Assistant Professor, Seoul National University, studied 48 depressed elderly patients. They used 61 age-matched controls. They exposed one group of subjects to a 4-week programme in a laughter group and another in a 4-week programme that did not involve laughter. They found that participants in the laughter group scored significantly lower on the Geriatric Depression Scale and higher on the Pittsburgh Sleep Quality Index.

Dr Malvash Shahidi and Dr Ali Mojtahad of the University of Teheran and the Khomeini Medical Centre, Teheran, Iran, respectively randomly assigned 60 community-dwelling depressed female elderly persons to a laughter yoga group, an exercise group and a control group. They found that the laughter group scored significantly higher than the other two groups on the Life Satisfaction Scale.

Table 4.3 below shows a list of some social benefits of laughter. Studies that claim support for some of these benefits are also cited.

TABLE 4.3 - SOCIAL BENEFITS OF LAUGHTER

	Benefit	Study by
1	Promotes Romance	E R Bessler
2	Reduces depression/tension	M Gelkopf
3	Promotes communication	I M Audette
4	Promotes bonding	
5	Aids learning and retention	
6	Reduces negative emotions	

Other claimed social benefits of laughter include increased altruism, looking younger and living longer. An article on the social benefits of humour or laughter published in This Emotional Life concludes: "Laughing out loud, being quietly amused, anticipating something funny and even forcing a smile or chuckle can all lead to increase in positive emotions and neutralise negative emotions which can help us to keep on the 'upward spiral' to greater happiness."

Eric Bressler of Westfield State College, Massachusetts, USA and Sigal Balshine of McMaster University, Hamilton, Ontario, Canada, had 200 male and female students examine photographs of males and females adults. Some of the adults had funny laughter-provoking captions next to them while, the controls had bland captions placed next to them. The students were asked who they would rather go out with. Most declared a preference for the adults with funny captions next to them.

Provine's theory that laughter promotes romance is used to explain the result of this study. 'Women are attracted to men who make them laugh,' Provine asserts. 'Men are attracted to women who laugh at their jokes,' said Provine. Girls beware. 'If you are not interested in a guy, do not laugh at his jokes.'

A study by Dr Marc Gelkopf, Associate Professor of Community Mental Health at the Faculty of Social Welfare and Health Services, University of Haifa, Haifa, Israel and fellow researchers showed that patients with schizophrenia following a laughter intervention achieved reduced hostility and depression/anxiety scores and increased activity and social competence scores.

How does laughter bring about social benefits? It does so indirectly. As stated earlier, laughter promotes the secretion of pain-reducing endorphins, stress-reducing and confidence-boosting serotonin and lowers the production of stressors such as cortisol and adrenaline. Reduction of pain and stress can produce the 'feel-good' factor. Laughter also promotes the increased supply of blood to organs especially the brain hence it can facilitate cerebral activities such as learning and memory. Therefore, we can conclude that physical benefits of laughter produce social dividends.

6. MISCELLANEOUS BENEFITS OF LAUGHTER

Other areas where benefits have been attributed to laughter are arthritis, diabetes, psycho-social illness and longevity.

a) Laughter and Arthritis

Norman Cousins' experience has been reported on. Pain reduction was the main benefit emphasised by this. However, Dr T Matsuzaki, Department of Joint Disease and Rheumatism, Nippon Medical School, Tokyo, Japan, and his colleagues, claimed another benefit for laughter in a study conducted by them. The subjects were 43 patients suffering from arthritis and 23 'healthy' adults. The levels of enzymes that fight against the factors that cause rheumatoid arthritis in the blood of the 66 subjects were measured before and after they had listened and laughed to Katungo, a traditional Japanese comic story. They found that the levels of the enzymes that fight rheumatoid arthritis rose in all the subjects. It rose significantly more in patients suffering from arthritis. They also reported that the more severe the arthritis, the higher the rise in the anti-inflammatory enzymes produced.

How does laughter reduce the pathological effects of arthritis? Enzymes called cytokines are known to be produced in connection with the disease rheumatoid arthritis. Pro-inflammatory cytokines worsen the condition. Anti-inflammatory cytokines fight the disease. Laughter is believed to decrease the amount of pro-inflammatory cytokines and increase the production of anti-inflammatory cytokines.

b) Laughter and Diabetes

Keiko Hayashi of the University of Tsukuba, Japan, led a study which found that laughter lowered the amount of blood sugar of 24 subjects. Nineteen of the subjects suffered from diabetes while five did not. The subjects were given identical meals and then had their blood sugar levels were measured before and after listening to 40 minutes of a monotonous lecture and listening and laughing to a Japanese comedy show. Blood sugar levels were lowered in all the subjects following their watching (and 'belly-laughing') during the comedy show.

c) Laughter and Genetics

T Hayashi (cited above) in a study analysed the changes induced by laughter on thousands of genes in the blood of patients with Type 2 diabetes. Their conclusion - "We demonstrated that laugther which is an expression of positive emotion is linked to gene expression". They cautioned, though, that the study, "does not allow reasonable interpretation for the regulation of gene expression by laughter". They recommend further study of the subject.

d) Laughter and Longevity

Dr Sven Svebak, Department of Neuroscience, Norwegian University of Science and Technology, Trondheim, Norway, and his colleagues tracked 54,000 Norwegians for 7 years. The individuals who found life funny (those who scored high on the Sense of Humour survey scale) lived 35% longer than those with low scores. In another study, the same researchers found that near-death patients who maintained a good sense of humour lived 31% longer than those who did not appreciate humour.

Reports by the American Cancer Society and the Montefiore Einstein Cancer Centre at Montefiore Hospital asserted that laughter promotes longevity. The reports added that, for maximum effect, the laughter needs to be supplemented with, wait for it, "moderate red wine and a handful of walnuts or peanuts'. Dr Howard Friedman, a Professor of Psychology at the University of California at Riverside provided an opposite view. He theorised that people who laugh a lot because of untempered optimism often indulge in risk-taking saying: "I'll be okay".

A CRITIQUE OF LAUGHTER STUDIES

Many observers of the effects of laughter claim that its health benefits are not based on sound research or that the positive effects are almost always exaggerated. Susan Brink of the National Geographic stated: 'The science backing up that (benefits of laughter) is thin. Most studies have been small and have relied on self-reported assessments'. Robert Provine (cited earlier) posited: "The definitive research into the potential health benefits of laughter just hasn't been done yet".

This was the contribution of Dr Erin Hamer of the Department of Health Psychology, Vanderbilt University, New York, to the discussion on the this subject: "Overall, there is no straightforward evidence that laughter has a particular effect on health. Some studies show promising results, only to not be replicated. Other studies show conflicting evidence." Then she added that people will go out to dinner with their friends, using a need to relax as an excuse to not do their homework. Laughter is a natural part of our lives, and is not going to cease from existence just because it has not been proven scientifically".

Just how does laughter benefit health? Is it the enjoyment of it? What is enjoyed is not always beneficial. Smoking, drinking and eating fried or fatty foods are examples. Is it the physical exercise aspect of it? Steve Wilson, a psychologist and laugh therapist seems to agree. He declared, "The effets of of laughter and exercise are very similar", he declared. "Combining laughter and movement …… is a great way to boost your heart rate".

Some researchers even lay emphasis on the negative effects of laughter. 'Who Says Laughter's the Best Medicine?' screamed the New York Times on December 20, 2013. The newspaper was reporting on the findings of a review of about 800 studies of laughter dating back to 1946. The reviewers were Dr Robin Ferner of the University of Birmingham and Dr Jeffrey Aronson from the Oxford University. Both are clinical pharmacologists with a special interest in medication errors. They found

85 studies that report the benefits of laughter, 114 studies that report 'harms' and 586 that 'deal with medical conditions' that have laughter as a symptom. Some critics even lay emphasis on some fatal outcomes of laughter. {See Appendix 6)

It is probably fair to say that Ferner and Aronson were expressing an irreverent view of the benefits of laughter. Their report also appeared in the Christmas edition of the British Medical Journal. Is it a case of yuletide jollity? There is a hint of that. Elizabeth Preston describes the reviewers as 'aspiring clowns' that 'can't resist throwing in a few puns of their own'.

Table 4.4 shows a list of some of the harms that laughter can cause.

TABLE 4.4 - PATHOLOGICAL RISKS OF LAUGHTER

Type of injury	Description
Respiratory	Inhalation of foreign bodies, inhalation of saliva, drink or food items, asthma attack, pneumothorax
Throat	Oesophageal rupture
Abdominal	Hernia
Central Nervous System	Headache Loss of will power that can lead to inability to take make rational decisions
Cardio-vascular System	Stroke

Musculo-skeletal System	Dislocation of the jaw Loss of muscle tone leading to cataplexy
Urinary System	Stress Incontinence

Laughter can result in death. 'He died laughing' is not completely meaningless. It must be noted that most of the deaths reported to be due to laughter are most probably due to pre-existing pathological conditions. Appendix 3 provides a list of deaths reported to be due to laughter.

Also, it must be remembered that most of the harms are rare and occur mostly during uncontrollable and prolonged belly laughter. As for the fatal consequences of laughter, pre-existing pathologies can be significant precipitating factors in the development of these harmful outcomes.

READING LIST

1. Cousins N (1979) Anatomy Of An Illness As Experienced By The Patient. Toronto: Bantam.
2. Dunbar R I et al Social laughter is correlated with an elevated pain threshold. *Proceedings of the Royal Society. London Series. B Biol Sci* 2012, 279: 1161 – 1167.
3. Berk L S et al, Neuro-endocrine and stress hormone changes during mirthful laughter. *American Journal of Medical Science*; 298(6): 390 – 6.
4. Chaya M S. Kataria M, Nagandra R (2008) The effects of hearty extended unconditional laughter using laughter Yoga techniques on physiological, psychological and immunological parameters in the workplace – a randomised

control trial. American Society of Hypertension, 2008 Annual Meeting May 14, 208. New Orleans, Louisiana, USA.

5. Cogan R et al (1987) Effects of laughter and relaxation on discomfort thresholds. *Journal of Behaviour Medicine*; 10 (2): 139 – 144.
6. Weisemberg M et al (1998) The influence of film-induced mood on pain perception. *Pain;* 76 (3) 365 – 375.
7. Bellert J L (1989) A therapeutic approach in oncology nursing. *Cancer Nursing;* 12, 2: 65 5- 70.
8. Erdman L (1991) Laughter therapy for patients with cancer. *Oncology Nursing Forum,* 18, 8 1359 – 1363.
9. Trent B (1990) Ottawa lodges add humour to armamentarium in fight against cancer. *Canadian Medical Association Journal,* 142(2): 163 – 164, 166.
10. Provine R R (2000) Laughing your way to health. *In: Provine R R A Scientific Evaluation*, New York, Viking, pp 189 – 207.
11. Martin R A (2001) Humour, laughter and physical health. Methodological issues and research findings. *Psychological Bulletin;* 127:504 – 519.
12. Bennett M P and Lengacher C A (2006) Humor and laughter may influence health. *Journal of Evidence-based Complementary and Alternative Medicine;* 3:61-3 [PMC] free article [PubMed].
13. Bessler E R and Balshine S (2006) Evolution and Human Behaviour. *Evolution;* 27: 29 – 39.
14. Gelkopf M, Kreitler S and Sigal M (1993) Laughter in a psychiatric ward. Somatic, emotional, social and clinical influences on schizophrenic patients. *Journal of Nervous Mental Diseases*, 181(3): 283 – 289.
15. Matsuzaki T, Nakajima, S, Ishigami M and Yoshino S (2006) Mirthful laughter differentially affects serum pro- and anti-inflammatory cytokine levels depending on the level of

disease activity in patients with rheumatoid arthritis. *Rheumatology 2006;* 45(2): 182 – 186.

16. Hayashi T and Murukami K (2009) The effects of laughter on post-prandial glucose levels and gene expression in Type 2 diabetic patients. *Life Sciences*; 85(5-6): 185 – 7.
17. Svebak S, Romundstad S and Holmen J (2010) A 7-year prospective study of sense of humour in an adult country population – the HUNT-2 study. *International Journal of Psychiatry in Medicine*; 40: 125 – 146.
18. Svebak S, Kristoffersen B and B Assarod K (2006) Sense of humour and survivor among a county cohort of patients with end-stage renal failure – a 2-year prospective study. *International Journal of Psychiatry in Medicine;* 36(3): 269 – 281.
19. Shahidi M and Mojtahad A (2001) Laughter Yoga versus group exercises programme in elderly depressed: a randomised controlled trial. *International Journal of Geriatric Psychiatry*; 26: 322 – 327.
20. Ferner R E and Aronson K (2013) Laughter and MIRTH (Methodological Investigation, Risibility, Therapeutic and Harmful): narrative synthesis. *BMJ,* 347: 7274.

CHAPTER 5
USE OF HUMOUR/LAUGHTER IN MEDICAL PRACTICE

One of the earliest Biblical references to laughter is recorded at Genesis 17. God told the patriarch, Abraham, that his wife, Sarah, will give birth to a son. Verse 17 says: 'At this Abraham fell facedown and began to laugh and to say in his heart: "Will a man 100 years old have a child born to him, and will Sarah, a woman 90 years old give birth?' Abraham most probably snickered. According to Chapter 18 verse 12, when Sarah overheard the discussion, she began to laugh to herself, saying: '…after I am worn out and my Lord is old, being advanced in years'.

Sarah, too, probably snickered.

This event took place some 4000 years ago. It did not have anything to do with laughter being considered medicinal. It was King Solomon who, about 1000 years later, became the first, according to Bible record, to credit humour or laughter with medical benefit. As mentioned earlier, he declared at Proverbs 17: 22 that 'a joyful heart is good medicine'. It is noticeable, though, that King Solomon cited some negative aspects of laughter and, therefore, cited some cautions with regard to it. A few examples are: there is time for laughter; it may be better to cry than to laugh at times; it is better to go the house of mourning than to a place of merriment.

Ancient Greek physicians believed that illnesses were due to an imbalance between 4 humours: black bile represented by the earth, yellow bile represented by the air, blood represented by fire and phlegm represented by water. According to the Greeks, diseases were the result of imbalance in the amount of these humours. Their physicians were known to discourage the use of medication to treat diseases. Rather, they used exercise and diet for the treatment of diseases. Also, notably, they prescribed for their patients to visit the halls of comedians. Laughter, the Greek believed could bring about a restoration of humoural balance to the body.

In the 14th century CE, Henri de Mondeville wrote; 'Let the surgeon take care to regulate the whole regimen of the patient's life for joy and happiness allowing his relatives and special friends to cheer him.'

Martin Luther, in the 16th century CE, used humour as part of his pastoral work. He advised depressed people who came to him to surround themselves with friends who would make them laugh.

Educator Richard Mulcator (born circa 1531), in Carlisle, Cumberland, Northern England and educated in Eton and Kings College, Cambridge, recommended the use of laughter for curing a head cold.

The German philosopher, Immanuel Kant, in the 18th century, used humour to restore emotional equilibrium.

The early parts of the 20th century witnessed the beginning of modern laughter therapy. A start was made in using clowns to cheer children with poliomyelitis admitted to US hospitals.

In recent times, 1964 to be more exact, Norman Cousins rekindled interest in the use of laughter for treating illnesses. In an article and later in a book, Cousin described how laughter helped in his recovery from ankylosing spondylitis. He replaced pain-killers with Vitamin C and watching Marx Brothers films and other TV sitcoms. Though Cousin's claim that it was laughter that cured him was heavily criticized, still, his account took over the consciousness of the American nation. This led to numerous articles about the physiology of laughter and its positive effects on health.

In 1972, Dr Hunter 'Patch' Adam founded the Gesundheit! Institution. This was a home-based free hospital to bring fun, friendship and joy to the sick.

USE OF LAUGHTER IN MEDICAL PRACTICE

Studies have made some interesting findings on the use of humour by doctors:

1. Patients' satisfaction increases when doctors, nurses and other medical professionals find time to 'chat' with them.

2. Complaints of malpractice leading to litigation are less when doctors, nurses and other medical professionals use humorous overtures to discuss deeper concerns with their patients.

Dr M Granek-Caterivas of the School of Continuing Education, Faculty of Medicine, Tel Aviv University, Tel Aviv, Israel, and other researchers conducted a cross-sectional study of two populations – doctors and patients in Israel. The purposes of the study were to find out the frequency of the use of humour or laughter in family practice and to qualitatively assess physicians' and patients' perception of the impact of the use of humour. Physicians reported that they used humour in 38% of their encounters with patients. Patients reported that humour was used in 60% of the encounters. The researchers' conclusion was that patients were 'more sensitised to humour than physicians'. Doctors seem to have the need to be more conscientious in the use of humour in their practice, whereas, their patients seem to expect it.

USE OF LAUGHTER BY NURSES

Nurses are the best placed of medical professionals to administer humour or laughter therapy. They have the longest and closest contact with the patients and their relatives, much more than any other medical professional. How can nurses best fulfil their role as laughter therapists? The following guidelines need to be followed:

1. Do not use laughter prematurely. First establish your professional competence.

2. Be sensitive to whether the patient is positive or negative about your sense of humour. Do not force humour on the patient.

3. Poke fun at yourself, never at the patient's or your colleagues' expense.
4. Never use laughter to deliver bad news.
5. Always take into consideration your patient's religious, cultural or socio-political views and his or her stress level or the severity of the illness.

USE OF LAUGHTER BY OCCUPATIONAL THERAPISTS AND PHYSIOTHERAPISTS

Kurt Hubbard, National Dean of the Occupational Therapy Assistant Associates Degree Programme at Remington College, Florida, USA, states: "Incorporating fun events and tasteful humor into (occupational therapy) will make the work less stressful and more enjoyable for everyone." That's saying the obvious, isn't it? Pursuant of this goal, Occupational Therapist J Vistnes of the Scepter Health and Rehabilitation Center, Atlanta, Georgia, USA described how the Occupational Therapy team used faked laughter sessions and or tug of war as part of their practice on a daily basis. As for the latter, 'the patients' team always wins', she stated.

Kristin Uppah, a Physical Therapist and graduate in Behavioural Neuroscience from St Ambrose University, Davenport, Iowa, USA, pleads with physiotherapists to apply to their practices the principles of 'collaboration, innovation and consumer centricity'. She added, in lay terms, that PTs should use the Medical Clowns principles. This is, again, a case of saying the obvious. Physiotherapists apply humour and laughter in their practice in various ways. Of course, more needs to be done to increase greater participation and enjoyment by clients and to reduce stress in themselves as practitioners.

USE OF HUMOUR OR LAUGHTER BY PARAMEDICS:

Some areas of medical care are characterised by dying and death. Intensive or Critical Care, Accident and Emergency and Terminal Care expose doctors and nurses to varying degrees of emotional stress. However, the area of paramedics providing first contact care for accident victims stands out as far as exposure to stress is concerned. In this setting, paramedics use humour and laughter to help them maintain morale, improve working relationships and ward off burn-out. They use mechanisms like drawing on past experience, ignoring stress and seeing the 'funny side of things'. This may seem to be incongruous, defying logic.

This type of humour has been dubbed as – 'Gallows Humour'. It has been noted that of all the major Theories of Humour, Freud's Relief Theory has the strongest association with Gallows Humour.

It is relevant to warn that patients should not be subjected to Gallows Humour. Patients could readily interpret it as uncaring, even cruel.

Studies also show that patients themselves use humour to cope with the anxiety associated with being in hospital. They ridicule hospital routines and their own lack of control of bodily functions. At times, patients bind together and socialise to take pleasure in group complaints about their care.

HUMOUR AND LEARNING

Humour and laughter are recognised as a facilitating tool for learning. Its positive impact is thought to be due to its power to gain and hold students' attention which is often difficult to do. Also, humour and laughter in the classroom tend to create a tension-free environment which raises students' interest.

Dr Ramesh Narula, Assistant Professor of Orthopaedics and his colleagues at the Rohilkhand Medical College, Bareilly , Uttra Pradesh, India, conducted a study to assess the effectiveness of humour when used in the teaching of medical students. They found that the use of humour led to statistically significant improvement in class attendance and the marks scored on testing. The conclusion of the researchers was that the use of humour or laughter in medical teaching leads to - 'sustainable, self-stimulating and positive learning'. 'Students adore teachers like that', they crowed. They then declared the following guidelines for using humour or laughter in the classroom:

1. Know your students.
2. Use humour appropriately.
3. Do not try too hard.
4. Include the whole class in the humour or laughter.

RECENT HISTORY OF LAUGHTER THERAPY

In 1964, Dr William F Fry, a professor of psychology at Stanford University, California, USA, published a report of his studies into the physiological effects of laughter. Other researchers, since then, have joined the effort to produce scientific evidence for the efficacy of laughter. Among these are, Dr Lee Berk, an immunologist at the Loma Linda University's School of Allied Health and Medicine, Dr Michael Miller, Director of the Center for Preventive Cardiology of the University of Maryland, Baltimore, USA and Japanese geneticist, Kazuo Murakumi. Murakumi demonstrated that laughter therapy can cut healthcare cost by 23%. This should be of special interest to healthcare providers all over the world especially in countries like Japan where the number of elderly people is rising inexorably.

The 'youngest' generation of proponents of laughter therapy are Mari Cruz Garcia Rodera, Spanish author and laughter enthusiast, Dr Madan Kataria, an Indian family doctor and Sebastien Gendry, a gelotologist and professional Laughter Therapist. It is worth noting that there are now two online laughter universities: A Laughter Yoga Online University founded by Dr Madan Kataria, which is based in Bangalore, India. The second is Laughter Online University founded in 2011 by Sebastien Gendry. It is based in Los Angeles, California, USA.

METHODS OF DELIVERING LAUGHTER THERAPY:

1. USE OF CLOWNS

Do you know that there are Clown Doctors? A professional Clown Doctors programme was launched in New York, USA, and now operates in Australia, New Zealand, Canada, Israel, all over Europe and indeed in most other parts of the world. Clown Doctors try to fill the psycho-social need of hospitalised children and, at times, adults. The techniques used include magic, parody, music, story-telling and other clowning skills to help children deal with a range of emotions – fear, anxiety, pain, loneliness and especially boredom.

Please note that Clown Doctors are not necessarily medical doctors. They are individuals, male or female, who have undergone advanced training in drama, entertainment and in the use of humour or laughter in medical settings. Of course, medical doctors can also play the role of clown doctors.

2. LAUGHTER ROOM

This is simply a room set aside for patients with their friends and relatives, if they wish, to get together to share jokes or watch funny movies and TV programmes. Books and comics may be provided. Clown doctors may use the room.

According to the Huffington Post, Washington's Sibley Memorial Hospital started to operate a Laughter café in 2012. Senior citizens have since been meeting there to laugh together. North Kansas City Hospital and Cancer Treatment Centers of America have similar programmes.

3. LAUGHTER YOGA

Laughter Yoga was started in 1995 by Dr Madan Kataria. On March 13, 1995, he held a laughter session in a park in Mumbai, India, with 5 persons. Over 6000 laughter clubs have since been established in over 65 countries. Eye contact and child-like playfulness are used to elicit laughter. The session is often concluded with laughter meditation while lying down or sitting in a yoga posture. Meditation and or spiritual enlightenment may be added to the session as appropriate.

The principles that underpin Yoga Therapy are:

a) Fake laughter, like genuine laughter, is beneficial.

b) Fake laughter can be easily converted to genuine laughter.

c) Laughter is contagious.

Is laughter yoga scientifically beneficial and valid? Ko and Youn (2011), conducted a study to investigate the effects of laughter yoga. The subjects of their study were 109 community-dwelling men and women over 65-years-old. They measured their pre and post-intervention sleep patterns and the levels of depression and cognition. The conclusion reached by the authors was: Laughter therapy is 'a useful, cost-effective and easily accessible intervention that has positive effects on depression, insomnia and sleep quality in the elderly'.

This book makes a distinction between Laughter exercise and Laughter Yoga. Laughter exercise involves straightforward exercise of the muscles that produce laughter. Yoga, on the other hand, often incorporates the adoption of special postures, meditation or even some form of spiritual experience.

4. LAUGHTER EXERCISE

The maxim, 'use it or lose it', applies to facial muscles as much as it does to other muscles of the body. Regular passive and active types of exercise are needed to maintain the suppleness and excitability and strength of facial muscles.

Other principles to be taken into consideration are:

a) The exercise of a muscle group is preferable to the exercise of each muscle in the group. Group exercise is more natural and time-efficient.

b) Warm-up is an essential part of the preparation for vigorous exercise.

c) Exercise against resistance is necessary for a muscle to be strengthened.

Facial massage is included in the Laughtercise regime partly to provide warm-up. However, there is a more important reason. Facial massage can facilitate a reduction of tension in facial muscles. Some researchers claim that it can reduce the rate of facial wrinkling due to ageing by 'firming up or plumping the skin over the face and around the neck.

In preparation for laughtercise, you should ensure a degree of privacy. If you want to be with others, be sure that they are people who will understand and accept the reasons for you to be making faces and or laughing at or by yourself'. Sitting in front of the mirror is the recommended position for Laughtercise. A laughtercise session should last about seven and a half to ten minutes.

1. Using the tips of your index and middle fingers of your dominant hand, lightly tap the skin over your forehead, around the eyes, over the nose, cheeks and chin.

2. Using the tip of the middle finger of your dominant hand, press down the skin over the central area of your forehead. Move the skin over the underlying bone of your forehead. Using small circular

movements work over your forehead, nose, around the eyes, over the cheeks and the chin.

3. Contort your face into a slight frown. Relax. Contort the face into a deeper frown. Relax. Contort the face into the deepest frown you can manage. Relax.
4. Using tips of your index finger and thumb of your dominant hand to hold your lips together, balloon your mouth. Relax. Make a bigger balloon. Relax. Make the biggest balloon you can manage. Relax.
5. Smile lightly. Relax. Smile broadly. Relax. Smile the widest you can.
6. Laugh a mild laugh. Relax. Laugh loudly. Relax. Laugh loudly until you are slightly breathless. Relax.

Warm down massage – Put the palm of your right hand on your forehead keeping the thumb separated from the other fingers. Sweep the hand over the left side of your face ensuring that the tip of your thumb moves between your left eye and the nose, over your upper lip to the right angle of your mouth. End the stroke by holding your chin between your thumb and index finger. Repeat the exercise using your left hand to massage the right side of your face. Repeat each exercise 3 times. You can massage each side 3 times or massage each side alternately 3 times.

HOW DO YOU FEEL?

TEN STEPS TO LAUGH MORE

1. Surround yourself with people who smile or laugh. Actively seek their company. (Rationale: Most of

laughter takes place in group settings. Laughter is contagious).

2. Smile at people – on the street, on the bus, at work, indeed at every opportunity. (Rationale: Smile at the world and the world will smile at you).

3. Try to change negative talk into positive. Dump moaners and complainers if you cannot change them. (Rationale: If you cannot beat them, don't join them).

4. Switch off the news on radio and TV. Read instead. Read funny books and funny parts of newspapers. (Rationale: depressing news depress laughter).

5. Watch funny movies – both modern and those of yore. (Rationale: Depressing news depress laughter).

6. Practice holding a straw between your front upper and lower teeth, not between your lips. This puts your face into a smiling expression. (Rationale: The brain responds to the sensation of smiling and assumes that laughter will ensue).

7. Practice laughing – in front of a mirror. If nobody is watching you, why worry? Produce laughter sounds – ha ha ha; hee hee hee. Make it longer; ha ha ha ha ha....; hee hee hee hee hee ..... Make it longer still, if you can. (Rationale: Practice makes perfect).

8. Do laughter exercise (laughtercise) – Massage your facial muscles and exercise them as described earlier in this chapter. (Rationale: Toning and firming up

facial muscles promote the tendency to smile and laugh).

9. Join a Laughter Class or Yoga Laughter Group – (Rationale: It is like joining a gymnasium or Exercise Class. Classmates can provide needed motivation for you).

10. Commit to smile and laugh. Commit to make others smile and laugh. Learn some jokes, witty quotes and funny stories. (Rationale: Laughter is contagious).

READING LIST

1. Bennett H J (Dec. 2003) Humor in Medicine. *Southern Medical Journal.*
2. Cho J (March 7, 1998) Laughter Therapy Takes Off in South Korea. *ABC News.*
3. MacDonald C (March 2004) A Chuckle a Day Keeps the Doctor Away. *Journal of Psychological Nursing and Mental Services.*
4. Robinson V M (1991) Humor of the Health Professions. Thorofare, New York, Slacks Inc. ed 2.
5. Cousins N (1979) Anatomy of an Illness as Perceived by the Patient: Reflections on Healing and Regeneration. New York, W W Norton.
6. Black D W (1984) Laughter. *Journal of the American Medical Association;* 252: 2995 – 2998.
7. Argyle M (1887) Is Happiness the Cause of Health? *Psychology of Health;* 12: 769 – 781.
8. Wender R C (1996) Humor in Medicine. *Primary Care*; 23: 141 = 154.

9. Segal D (1984) Playing Doctors, seriously: Graduation follies at an American Medical School. *International Journal of Health Services;* 14: 379 – 396.

10. Cushner F D and Friedman R J (1989). Humor and the Physician. *Southern Medical Journal;* 82: 51 – 52.

11. Narula D R, Chaudhary D V, Agarwal D A and Narula D K (2011) Humor As a Learning Aid in Medical Education. *National Journal of Integrated Research Medicine,* 2(1): 22 -24.

12. Kenneth C Kelman (2001) A Study of Story-telling, Humor and Learning in Medicine. *Clinical Medicine;* 1(3) 1222 – 1232.

13. Alexander D A and Klein S (2003) Ambulance Personnel and critical Incidents: Impact of Accident and emergency work on mental health and emotional well-being. *British Journal of Psychiatry;* 178(1) 76 - 81.

14. Beck C T (1997) Humor in Nursing Practice: a Phenomenological Study. *International Journal of Nursing Studies;* 34(5) 346 – 352.

15. Charman S (2013) Have You Heard the One About the Emergency Services' Joke-book? *Ambulance Today;* (Autumn 2013) 41 – 43.

16. Griner P F (2013) Burnout in healthcare providers. *Journal of Integrative Medicine*; 12(1) 22 – 24.

17. Kuiper N A (2012) Humor and Resiliency: Towards a Process Model of Coping and Growth. *Europe's Journal of Psychology;* 8(3) 475 – 491.

CHAPTER 6
THERAPY AND MEDICAL JOKES

Question by Physiotherapy tutor: What is the name the main bone of the upper arm?

Physiotherapy student: The humorous.

⋆⋆⋆

Patient to physiotherapist as she (the patient) pokes her right side with her index finger: I feel pain here and here and here. She pokes her right knee and hip.

Physiotherapist: Is that it?

Patient, poking the same finger into her left side and back: And here and here.

Physiotherapist: You have a sore finger.

⋆⋆⋆

Physiotherapist to overweight patient: What fits your schedule better - exercising for 1 hour a day or being dead 24 hours a day?

⋆⋆⋆

Physiotherapist to golf enthusiast: I can certainly improve the movement in your injured shoulder. I'm afraid I cannot improve your handicap.

⋆⋆⋆

Patient giving a history to physiotherapist: I was doing the hokey pokey two weeks ago. I put my left hip in and I put the right one out. It has stayed there since then.

★★★

Physiotherapist to obese patient: Does obesity run in your family?

Patient: Nobody runs in my family.

★★★

A hand-written sign seen at the door of a private Physiotherapist who specialises in Manual manipulation: I'll be back in a snap.

★★★

Ten Rules of Physiotherapy (courtesy of Frederick Zappone).

1. Never say: "I can't." You'll be made to do it anyway.
2. Never say: "It's easy." It'll be made harder.
3. Never say: "I've lost count." You'll have to start all over again.
4. Never say: "This is taking too long." You'll stay longer.
5. Never complain. They never listen.
6. Never argue. They always win.
7. Never wince or scream. This encourages them.
8. Never say or look like you are enjoying it. They'll stop it.

9. Never hold your breath even when you are asked to do so. If you faint or DIE they have to do a lot of paperwork.

10. Never cheat. You'll regret it.

★★★

From physiotherapists' notes:

1. Patient has chest pain when he lies on his left side for a year.
2. This lady slipped on the ice and apparently her legs went their separate ways.
3. There is numbness from the toes down.
4. He suffers from occasional constant pins and needles in his fingers.

★★★

What is the difference between a terrorist and a physiotherapist?

You can negotiate with a terrorist.

★★★

NURSES JOKES:

Who is a nurse?

A nurse is an angel living among humans.

★★★

What is the difference between Mother Theresa and a nurse?

Mother Theresa worships only one God.

★★★

A nurse that smiles when things are going wrong in the ward is surely going off duty.

★★★

Friend to a student nurse: When are you free to hang about?

Student nurse: In three years' time.

★★★

Nurse to a loud cheeky male patient: Mr Smith, who chooses the size of your catheter?

Mr Smith: (Silence).

★★★

Nurse Susan is helping a patient who is a physiotherapist to the bathroom. Nurse Alice meets them in the corridor.

Nurse Alice, beaming and shouting for the whole ward to hear: Susan, do unto him as he does unto others.

DOCTOR JOKES

Doctor to patient – Laughter is the best medicine; which is fortunate as laughter is all our healthcare plan now offers.

★★★

What did the doctor dictate? What did the secretary type?

1. This patient presents with *sick as hell disease* – (Sickle cell disease).

2. This 40-year old *occasional* male ..... – (Caucasian male).
3. Patient presents with pancreatitis of unknown *ideology* – (aetiology).
4. This gentleman has a respe*ctable* cancer of the liver – (resect- able).
5. Mr Smith is a professional tennis player. He presents with acute pain in his right *old crayon* process – (0lecranon process).
6. This young lady has been suffering from *grandma* seizures for three years – (grand mal).
7. This elderly man presents with *fleas bite his left leg......* (phlebitis of his left leg*)*.
8. Mr Brown had a *baloney* amputation last year .... (below knee).
9. While in A and E, Mrs Green was *x-rated* and sent home because..... (x-rayed).
10. This patient was discharged home with a month's supply of *Lanzarote ..... (lanzaprazole)*.

Typos

1. One doctor to another: I saw your patient today. He is doing well under the *car* of our physiotherapist.
2. Pathology report: *Lover* Function Test is normal.
3. Sign above a Gynaecologist's clinic – Dr Jones, at your *cervix*.
4. From a medical note: Examination of this gentleman's genitalia reveals that he is *circus-sized*.

These are not typos. What are they? Brain slips?

1. This patient has been depressed ever since she began to see me in 2010.
2. The patient was discharged without permission.
3. This healthy-looking decrepit 80-year-old male is alert but forgetful.
4. This patient has no history of suicide.
5. Gynaecologist, referring a patient to an endocrinologist: Between you and I, we should be able to get this lady pregnant.
6. This 79-year-old widow no longer lives with her husband.
7. On admission to the ward, her rapid heart stopped and she is feeling much better now.
8. The baby was delivered, the cord was clamped and cut. The baby was handed to the obstetrician. He breathed and started to cry immediately.
9. This gentleman had his left foot amputated six months ago. The left leg was amputated at the knee two years ago.
10. This lady was transferred from the Accident and Emergency to the ward without dressing.

★ ★ ★

General Practitioner to 7-year-old Timmy: The difference between me and your mum is that I went to medical school but your mum went to Google. Who do you believe?

Timmy: My mummy!

★★★

Doctor to patient: I remember you! You paid your last bill with a counterfeit cheque.

Patient: Oh yes. That was for the false medical certificate you gave me.

★★★

Patient to doctor: Doctor, I feel funny.

Doctor: Funny how?

Patient: I don't know. I just feel funny.

Doctor: Ok. Tell me a joke. I'll tell you if you are funny or not.

★★★

Doctor to patient: I have good news for you.

Patient: Yes?

Doctor: You are the healthiest patient in the Critical Care Unit.

★★★

Patient to surgeon: I need a brain replacement.

Surgeon: No problem. A male brain will cost you £10,000, while a female will cost about £5,000.

Patient: Why the difference?

Surgeon: The male brain has never been used.

★★★

Friend to friend: The doctor asked me to avoid all forms of stress. So I have not opened his bill.

★★★

Doctor to patient, while listening to stomach sounds of the patient complaining of indigestion:

I can hear a power struggle between spaghetti and pickled onion.

★★★

Patient to doctor: I'll not insult you by offering you payment.

Doctor: May I have the prescription I just gave you. I just want to make a little adjustment.

★★★

Patient to Orthopaedic Surgeon: I think I've broken my leg in two places.

Orthopaedic surgeon: I think you should stop going to those places.

★★★

Ear, Nose and Throat Doctor to patient: Miss James, please open your mouth wide. Now say Ahhh.

Miss Jones: Why? Why should I be saying Ahhh, Ahhh. Ok, Ahhhhhhhhhhhh…

★★★

Doctor to patient who is worried about his high blood pressure: Stop taking every instruction I give you with a pinch of salt.

★★★

Surgeon to patient: Do you want a local anaesthetic?

Patient: No. I prefer an imported one.

★★★

Doctor to patient: Are you on HRT?

Patient: No. I'm on Income Support.

★★★

EXERCISE JOKES

Doctor to obese patient who is finding it difficult to lose weight: But I told you to double your activity level.

Patient: I sure did. I have been using both hands to turn on the TV.

★★★

Doctor to obese patient: Turning the handle on your recliner chair does not count as an exercise on a rowing machine.

★★★

Obese gentleman to doctor: Doctor, can you please prescribe something to stop me from sleep-walking.

Doctor: No. You need the exercise.

★★★

Lady on the phone to gymnasium receptionist: What do you mean 'wear loose-fitting clothing'? If I had loose-fitting clothing will I be wanting to come to your gym?'

★★★

Receptionist at a gymnasium to a lady on the phone:

You want to lose a pound?

"......."

Did you say right now?

"....."

Ok. Now, press '1' on your telephone pad eighteen thousand times.

" ....."

Hello. Hello. Are you there?

★★★

Overheard:

1. I exercised once and found that I am allergic to it. My skin got flushed, my heart raced away and I got short of breath. Exercise is too dangerous for me.
2. I thought of exercise but ate a cake and took a nap instead. It is the thought that counts, isn't it?
3. Exercise would be so much more rewarding if calories screamed as you burn them.
4. I try to exercise first thing in the morning before my brain figures out what I am doing.
5. I finally decided to go out jogging. I heard clapping behind me. From my .... (Work it out yourself).
6. I just had to stop jogging. My thighs kept rubbing together. I didn't want to set my underwear on fire.
7. I don't exercise. Lest, I spill my coffee.

8. Lady to a Travel Agent: I want a place hot enough to melt the fat the moment I step on to the beach.

Obese man to doctor: I try to eat healthy. I never put salt on ice cream; I eat only decaffeinated pizza and my beer is free of fat.

Husband to wife: I am apple-shaped. You are pear-shaped. How much healthier can we be? Broccoli-shaped?

Elderly man to an elderly lady friend: I've been taking this medication for over 20 years. It is making me fat. It's giving me wrinkles and now I am bald. I'm going to sue.

One over-weight man to another: I spend over 45 minutes a day on the exercise bike. Next week I may try turning the pedal.

Wife returning from work to husband who has been home all day: How did the day go?

Husband: Very well indeed!

Wife surveying the mess all over the house: Yes?

Husband: Oh y e s! For 30 minutes, I looked for my jogging bottoms; for 25 minutes I looked for my trainers. I then spent 5 minutes on the treadmill. I have been warming down since then.

★★★

Wife to husband: You are back! You went out to jog just five minutes ago!

Husband: I forgot something.

Wife: What?

Husband: I forgot that I am not fit.

★★★

Why did the lady name her dog 'Miles'?

So that she can say that she walks miles every day.

★★★

CHAPTER 7
MISCELLANEOUS JOKES

CHANGING A LIGHT BULB

1. How many physiotherapists does it take to change a light bulb?

None. Physiotherapists do not change light bulbs. They exercise them until they get better.

2. How many occupational therapists will it take to change a light bulb?

None. The bulb will be taught a new occupation.

3. How many osteopaths are needed to change a light bulb?

One. It will take 9 visits, though.

4. How many nurses will it take to change a light bulb?

Two. One to change the bulb and another to write the report.

5. How many doctors are needed to change a light bulb

None. They ask the nurses to do it.

6. How many lawyers are needed to change a light bulb?

Two. One to move the motion to change the bulb, the other to stand up and shout: 'Objection, my Lord!'

7. How many psychologists are needed to change a light bulb?

One. Just that the bulb must first agree to change.

8. How many medical students will it take to change a light bulb?

One. It will take five years, though.

9. How many graduates are needed to change a light bulb?

Five. One to get on a chair to change the bulb, four to take the chair away from under him or her.

10. How many astronomers does it take to change a light bulb?

None. They prefer to watch in the dark.

11. How many bureaucrats are needed to change a light bulb?

Ten. One to change the bulb and 9 to write reports about how to or not to change a bulb.

12. How many Einsteins will it take to change a bulb?

Unknown. It is all relative, isn't it?

13. How many TV evangelists are needed to change a light bulb?

Just one. Just that he collects donations first.

14. How many pigmies are needed to change a light bulb?

Three. (Think about the small matter of size).

When a doctor's wife eats an apple a day what happens?

She lives a lonely life.

★★★

Name 3 life-changing apples.

Adam and Eve's apple, Newton's apple and Steve Job's apple.

★★★

'Always give a 100% or don't give at all', a group of medical students are told.

'Does that apply to giving blood?' a student asks.

★★★

A man desperate for a job, any job, approaches a zoo keeper. He is offered a job which involves being in a cage dressedg up as a gorilla and entertaining visitors.

He enjoys eating bananas and beating his chest before the crowd until one day a lion is put in the same cage. The lion makes threatening thrusts towards the gorilla. 'I am not a gorilla,' it starts to scream.

'Keep your voice down. Better still, shut up!' the lion says. 'I'm not a lion either.'

★★★

An elderly lady using a Zimmer Frame to another lady also with a Zimmer Frame: The problem with the young generation is that they just cannot stand on their own two feet.

★★★

DEFT DEFINITIONS:

Facial exercise: Poor man's plastic surgery.

Calories: Little creatures that lurk in the wardrobe and sew clothes a little bit tighter every night.

★ ★ ★

A tip to reduce weight: Turn your head to the right. Then quickly turn it to the left. Do this 5 times. Repeat the exercise every time you are offered something to eat.

★ ★ ★

ANATOMICAL CHIT-CHATS

It is going tibia ok.

That is terrific, simply fibula.

I ulna be with you.

Lock the door; lest thieves radius.

★ ★ ★

Question: Who said this? If you fall, I'll be there for you.

Answer: The Floor.

★ ★ ★

What does a bathroom scale do?

It shows you the numerical value of your relationship with gravity.

★ ★ ★

One woman to another: We women never admit our age.

Other woman: Men never act theirs.

⋆⋆⋆

Young woman returning home from maternity ward with twins:

'I bought one and got one free.'

⋆⋆⋆

Friend to another friend

1st friend: We are best friends, aren't we?

2nd friend: I know.

1st friend: If you fall, I'll pick you up. Do you know?

2nd friend: I know. I know.

1st friend: When I finish laughing.

⋆⋆⋆

Serious-looking lady to her giggling friend:

Ok ok. Stop laughing so I can tell you the joke.

⋆⋆⋆

Answers to Medical Examination questions.

What is?

1. Antibody	Hatred towards one's own body.
2. Artery	Study of fine arts.
3. Bacteria	The back-door to a cafeteria.
4. Cardiology	Advanced study of playing cards.
5. Coma	Punctuation mark.

6. Exercise Therapy	Ability to use one's own judgement
7. Gall bladder	A girl's bladder.
8. Genes	Denim trousers.
9. Homeostasis	Drinking while you are peeing.
10. Kinesiology	Study of motion pictures
11. Labour pain	To be hurt at work.
12. Liposuction	A type of French kiss.
13. Ultrasound	Radical sound.
14. Relativity	Waiting for a late bus/train; 5 minutes feels like an hour. Waiting for a date; an hour feels like 5 minutes. That is relativity.

★★★

What is the best excuse for bad writing?

I am a doctor.

What is the worst excuse for bad writing?

I am a calligraphist.

★★★

Good advice:

1. Don't drive; instead, ride a bike – a bike runs on fat and saves you money; a car runs on money and makes you fat.
2. Stay calm. Remember that if plan A fails, there are 25 more letters of the alphabet.

★★★

What is a conclusion…when you are tired of thinking.

★★★

One clergy man to another:

I used to think that I had super power until I went to the physiotherapist.

★★★

A young lady to another young lady:

What do you mean I suffer from insanity? I enjoy every moment of it.

★★★

A young lady, feeding back to her father after her visit to the GP:

My doctor asked me to start killing people.

Her mother: Daisy! The doctor didn't say anything like that. He said that you should reduce the stress in your life.

Young lady: Same thing, innit?

★★★

Married men think that bachelors are lucky. Bachelors think that married men are the lucky ones. The problem is that married men think during the day; bachelors think at night.

★★★

Precocious frisky child to mother: Mum, What if I am kidnapped?

Mum: Believe you me, they'll bring you back, swiftly.

★★★

The changing pattern of exams:

1940s	Answer all the questions.
1960s	Answer any five of the ten questions.
1980s	Tick the correct answer, A, B or C.
2020s	Write your own question and answer it.
2050s	Thank you for turning up. You passed!!!

★★★

How does an Israelite make his tea?

Hebrews it.

★★★

A man takes his wife and mother-in-law on a holiday to Palestine. The mother-in-law dies during the holiday. The undertaker informs the man that burial in the holy land will cost the equivalent of £1000 sterling. The alternative, repatriation of the body to the UK, will cost £5000 sterling. The man chooses repatriation to the UK. He was asked why.

His reply: A man died and was buried here. And he was resurrected! Im not taking that chance!

★★★

What is the difference between a psychotic and a neurotic?

A psychotic believes that 3 +3 = 8 and does not worry about it.

A neurotic knows that 3 + 3 = 6 but worries about it.

★★★

From the Tax Office: We've got all it takes to take all you've got.

★★★

Captain Spock: Very funny, Scotty; now beam my clothes up.

★★★

One woman to another: Now that I've let the cat out of the bag please help me to put it back in.

★★★

Parishioner to her priest: Money doesn't buy happiness? Tell HIM to give me a chance to prove it.

★★★

Lady to psychic: You're asking for my name?

★★★

Man to man: There are two theories about arguing with a woman. Neither works.

★★★

One work-mate to another: You're are asking me for help? I'm busier than a one-toothed man in a corn-on-the cob eating competition.

★★★

One obese lady to another obese lady: I get my exercise by pushing my luck.

★★★

Car mechanic to car owner - I couldn't fix your brakes, so I made the horn louder.

★★★

Quite confusing:

If love is blind, what is love at first sight?

Why call a house a building when it has already been built?

If money does not grow on trees, why do banks have branches?

Can one cry under water?

Does a fish get thirsty?

Why call it 'rush hour' when nothing moves?

If waiting is good for health, how come waiters don't live forever?

A whale swims all day long, eats only fish, yet it is fat.

A rabbit eats only vegetables, runs and hops all day, yet it lives only five years! A tortoise does not even run and it lives for 150 years.

Why do people who rob banks go to jail while banks who rob people give their managers bonuses?

Why is common sense not common?

You can pee without pooing. You cannot poo without peeing. Why?

If you succeed to fail, have you failed or succeeded?

★★★

Ill-advised: Don't break another person's heart. He or she has only one. Break one of his or her bones instead. The person has 206.

★★★

That is serious:

1. If you are laughing when everyone is serious.
2. If everyone is laughing when you are serious.

★★★

Have you got a Mathematical problem? Phone 020tanB-CosC –x(B-A) for help.

CHAPTER 8
QUOTABLE QUOTES

A] 100 LAUGHTER OR HUMOUR QUOTES

1. Even the gods love a joke - Plato
2. The art of medicine consists of amusing the patient while nature cures the disease - Voltaire
3. What soap is to the body, laughter is to the soul – Jewish proverb.
4. Glee is legal, free and non-fattening – Song by Huey Lewis.
5. If you can laugh at it, you can survive it – Bill Cosby.
6. Laughter brings out the child in all of us – Bill Cosby.
7. A day without laughter is a day wasted – Charlie Chaplin.
8. He laughs best who laughs last – Sir John Vanbrugh.
9. He who laughs lasts – Mary Pettibone Poole.
10. Laughter is the tonic, the relief, the surcease for pain – Charlie Chaplin.

11. You can tell how smart people are by what they laugh at – Tina Fey.
12. Seven days without laughter makes one weak – Mort Walker.
13. The most wasted day is that on which we have not laughed – Sebastian Rich Nicholas Chamfort.
14. I got sacked from my last job for laughing. Mind you, I was driving the hearse at the time – Neil Baxter.
15. To jealousy nothing is more frightful than laughter – Francoise Sagan.
16. There is little success where there is little laughter – Andrew Carnegie.
17. The human race has one really effective weapon and that is laughter – Mark Twain.
18. We do not laugh because we are happy. We are happy because we laugh – William James.
19. Laugh and the world laughs with you. Snore and you sleep alone – Anthony Burgess.
20. Laughter has no foreign accent – Paul Lowney.
21. It is impossible to be angry and laugh at the same time. You have the power to choose either – Wayne Dyer.
22. I do not trust anyone who doesn't make me laugh – Maya Angelou.
23. Holding on to anger and hurt only gives you tense muscles, a headache and a sore jaw from

clenching your teeth. Forgiveness gives you back the laughter and the lightness of your life – Joan Lunden.

24. Even if there is nothing to laugh about laugh in credit – Anonymous.
25. When people are laughing they are generally not killing one another – Alan Alda.
26. A good cry is a wet wash; a good laugh is a dry cleaning – Adapted.
27. Sometimes a laugh is more important than food – Adapted.
28. A good laugh recharges your batteries – Adapted.
29. We do have a zeal for laughter in most situations give or take a dentist – Joseph Heller.
30. Laughter is a tranquiliser with no side effects – Arnold Glasow.
31. A laugh is a smile that bursts - Mary H Waldrip.
32. Good food, a good laugh and a long sleep are the best cures in the doctor's book – Irish Proverb.
33. We are paying a high price for taking life too seriously. Now Is the time to take laughter seriously – Dr Madan Kataria.
34. Laughter is the sun that drives winter from the human face – Victor Hugo.
35. If you laugh a lot, when you get old your wrinkles will be in the right places – Unknown Author.

36. Our life begins with our own cry. It ends with others' cry. Try to fill the gap with as much laughter as possible – Unknown Authur.
37. If you can make a girl laugh you can make her do anything – Marilyn Monroe.
38. Love is the treasure. Laughter is the key – Yakov Smirnoff.
39. Everybody laughs the same in every language because laughter is a universal connection - Yakov Smirnoff.
40. Laughter isn't a sign of insanity but a shield against it – Richelle E Goodrich.
41. If you want to tell people the truth make them laugh first, otherwise they'll kill you – Oscar Wilde.
42. Laughter is the sound of the soul dancing. My soul probably looks like Fred Astaire – Jarod Kintz.
43. Dogs laugh with their tails. Man is higher. He laughs at the other end – Adapted.
44. A man isn't poor if he can still laugh – Raymond Hitchcock.
45. A good time to laugh is anytime you can – Linda Ellerbe.
46. Man, when you lose your laugh you lose your footing – Ken Kesey.
47. A grand-child's laughter is the greatest medicine – A grand father.

48. No man who has once heartily and wholly laughed can be altogether irreclaimably bad – Thomas Carlyle.

49. Laughter is an orgasm triggered by the intercourse between sense and non-sense – Unknown Author.

50. Laughter is God's hand on the shoulder of a troubled world – Bettenell Huntznicker.

51. A smile is the cheapest face lift – Unknown Author.

52. Everything is funny when you are forbidden to laugh – Unknown Author.

53. Laughter does not have to be yours to heal – Unknown Author.

54. Laughter is when a smile has an orgasm – Unknown Author.

55. Laughter is the fireworks of the soul – Josh Billings.

56. Laughter is the sensation of feeling good all over and showing it principally in one place – Josh Billings.

57. You cannot deny laughter; when it comes, it flops down in your favourite chair and stays as long as it wants – Stephen King.

58. Through the window yesterday I saw a fool talking to himself and it made me laugh until I realized that it was a mirrored window – Jarod Kuntz.

59. Laughter is the most civilized music in the world - Unknown Author.
60. Laughter is inner jogging – Norman Cousin.
61. My favourite kind of pain is in my stomach, when my friends make me laugh too hard - Yuki K.
62. Live to laugh and laugh to live - James Isildor Nyaaba.
63. Laugh whenever you can. Keeps you from killing yourself when things are bad. That and vodka - Jim Butcher.
64. Among those who I like or admire I can find no common denominator but among those whom I love I can: all of them make me laugh - W H Auden.
65. I know not all that may be coming but be it what it will, I'll go to it laughing - Herman Melville.
66. It was her habit to build laughter out of inadequate material - John Steinbeck.
67. I'd rather laugh with sinners than cry with the saints - Billy Joel.
68. Laughter is America's most important export - Walt Disney Company.
69. You have as much laughter as you have faith - Martin Luther.
70. It is cheerful to God when you laugh from the bottom of your heart - Martin Luther King.

71. Those who don't know how to weep with their whole heart do not know how to laugh either - Golda Meir.

72. They all laughed when I said I'd become a comedian. Well, they are not laughing now - Bob Monkhouse.

73. When was the last time you had a good-belly-shaking-tear-jerking-snot-producing laugh? Yes, that long - Osayi Osar Emokpae.

74. Laughter is the only medicine without side effects - Shannon L Alder.

75. He had an idea that even when beaten he could steal a little victory by laughing at defeat - John Steinbeck.

76. Laughter is just like champagne – only without the headache afterwards - Elizabeth Jane Howard.

77. Life is short. Smile while you still have teeth - Sheila Cottrell.

78. Sexiness wears thin, beauty fades but to be married to a man who makes you laugh every day, ah, now, that's a treat - Joanne Woodward.

79. Italians make you laugh and then break your heart - Chloe Thurlow.

80. Nigerians break your heart and then make you laugh - (This author).

81. There are some things so serious you have to laugh at them - Niels Bohr, Nuclear Physicist.

82. Beware of those who laugh at nothing or everything - Arnold H Glasgow.
83. Laugh about the past; dream about the future - Rosemary Wixom.
84. Laughter is loudest where the food is the best - Irish proverb.
85. Man makes plans; God laughs –Michael Chabon.
86. Count your age by the number of your friends. Count your life by your smiles not tears – John Lennon.
87. As soon as you have made a plan, laugh at it – Lao Tzu.
88. It is bad to suppress laughter. It goes back down and spreads to your hips – Fred Allen.
89. A smile is a curve that sets everything straight – Phyllis Diller.
90. He that is of a merry heart has a continual feast – Proverbs 15: 15.
91. I commend laughter – Ecclesiastes 8: 15.
92. God has a laugh on his face – Psalm 42: 5.
93. A balanced person is one who finds both sides of an issue laughable – Herbert Procknow.
94. Cancer is probably the un-funniest thing in the world but I'm a comedian and even cancer couldn't stop me from seeing the humour in what I went through – Gilda Radner

95. The greatest prayer that you can pray is to laugh every day – Ramtha.
96. An optimist laughs to forget, a pessimist forgets to laugh – Tom Nansbury.
97. I make myself laugh at everything for fear of having to weep at it – Pierre-Augustin Caron de Beuamarchais.
98. To laugh at men of sense is the privilege of fools – Jean de La Bruyere.
99. Always leave people laughing when you say Goodbye – George Michael Cohan.
100. I believe that laughter is the best emotional Band-Aid in the world. It is like nature's Neosporin – Matt LeBlanc.

50 HAPPINESS QUOTES

1. Happiness is an inside job - William Arthur Ward.
2. Happiness is when what you think, what you say and what you do are in harmony - Mahatma Gandhi.
3. Real happiness is cheap enough yet how dearly we pay for its counterfeit - Hosea Ballou.
4. People don't notice whether it is winter or summer when they are happy - Anton Chekhov.
5. Happiness is solid; joy is liquid - J D Salinger.

6. The three essentials of happiness are something to do, something to hope for and something to love - Joseph Addison.
7. Happiness is like a kiss. You must share it to enjoy it - Bernard Meltzer.
8. If you want to be happy, be - Leo Tolstoy.
9. Happiness is not a goal; it is a by-product - Eleanor Roosevelt
10. We are no longer happy as soon as we want to be happier - Walter Savage Landor.
11. Anything in large doses is gonna kill you. Even happiness - Sandra Bullock
12. He who avoids complaint invites happiness - Abu Bakr.
13. Success is getting what you want. Happiness is liking what you get - H Jackson Brown Jnr.
14. Choose your life's mate carefully. From this one decision will come 90 per cent of all your happiness or misery - H Jackson Brown Jnr.
15. There is no way to happiness. Happiness is the way - Thich Nhat Hanh.
16. The best cosmetic for beauty is happiness - Unknown author.
17. Happiness is a good bank account, a good cook and a good digestion - Jean-Jacques Rousseau.
18. Happiness is the natural flower of duty - Phillips Brooks.

19. Man only likes to count his troubles; he doesn't calculate his happiness - Fyodor Dostoyevsky.

20. Now and then it's good to pause in our pursuit of happiness and just be happy - Guillaume Appolinaire.

21. I'd far rather be happy than be right any day - Douglas Adams.

22. A mathematical formula for happiness: Happiness (H) = Reality (R) divided by Expectation (E). [H = R/E). There are two ways to be happy: Increase your reality or lower your expectation - Jodi Picoult.

23. Whoever is happy will make others happy - Anne Frank.

24. Got no cheque books; got no banks. Still I'd like to express my thanks. I've got the sun in the morning and the moon at night – Irvin Berlin.

25. Money may not buy happiness but I'd rather cry in a Jaguar than in a bus – Francoise Sagan.

26. A large income is the best recipe for happiness I ever heard of – Jane Austen.

27. It is a kind of spiritual snobbery that makes people think that they can be happy without money – Albert Camus.

28. There is more happiness in giving than there is in receiving – Acts 20: 35.

29. The gratification of desire is not happiness - Daisaku Ikeda.

30. One of Satan's most frequently used deceptions is that the commandments of God are meant to restrict freedom and limit happiness – Ezra Taft Benson.
31. But happiness is no respecter of persons – Stephen Fry.
32. The British do not expect happiness. I had the impression all the time I lived there that they do not want to be happy; they want to be right – Quentin Crisp.
33. The search for happiness is one of the chief sources of unhappiness – Eric Hoffer.
34. Nothing flatters a man as much as the happiness of his wife; he is always proud of himself as the source of it – Samuel Johnson.
35. The health of the people is really the foundation upon which all their happiness and all their power as a state depends – Benjamin Disraeli.
36. In friendship as well as love, ignorance very often contributes more to happiness than knowledge – Francois de La Rochefoucauld.
37. Happiness in intelligent people is the rarest thing I know – Ernest Hemmingway.
38. Do not speak of your happiness to one less fortunate than yourself – Plutarch.
39. Happiness is a warm gun – John Lennon.

40. We have no more right to consume happiness without producing it than to consume wealth without producing it- George Bernard Shaw.

41. Happiness is an imaginary condition formerly often attributed to the dead now usually attributed by adults to children and by children to adults – Thomas Szasz.

42. To forget oneself is to be happy – Robert Louis Stevenson.

43. I think happiness is what makes you pretty. Period. Happy people are pretty – Drew Barrymore.

44. I am a kind of paranoid. I suspect people of trying to make me happy – T D Salinger.

45. Happiness is like a cloud; if you stare at it long enough it evaporates – Sarah McLachlan.

46. The two enemies of happiness are pain and boredom – Arthur Schopenhauer.

47. A table, a chair, a bowl of fruits and a violin, what else does a man need to be happy? - Albert Einstein.

48. Happy is he who bears what he cannot change – Friedrich Schiller.

49. One is never as unhappy as one thinks nor as happy as one hopes – Duc de la Rochefoucauld.

50. It is only possible to live happily ever after, one day at a time – Margaret Wander Bonanno.

HAPPINESS IS

1. …being able to do what people say that you cannot do.
2. …accepting that you don't have to be like everyone and that everyone doesn't have to be like you.
3. …being at the bottom of the ladder you want to be on rather than at the top of the ladder you do not like to be on.
4. …refusing to allow past mistakes determine your future.
5. …a bad memory.
6. …fashioning a smile out of tears.
7. …getting more than you expected.
8. …admiring without desiring.
9. …leisurely breakfast.
10. …waking up and finding out that one still has one hour to sleep.
11. …expecting an injection but getting a tablet instead.
12. …being able to use the toilet un-interrupted in a one bed-room house with six children.
13. …answering the phone and finding that the person on the other side is not a PPI caller.
14. …a contagious smile.
15. …being content with where and what you are.
16. …paying the last instalment of a loan.

17. …watching your son or daughter cut up his or her credit card.
18. …getting a rebate from the tax man (i.e getting blood from a stone).
19. …laughing first thing in the morning.
20. …knowing that your student is learning something.
21. …feeling the warm ocean breeze while lying on the beach on a hot day... ahhhhh!
22. …looking at a sleeping child.
23. …listening to a child laughing.
24. …hearing the sound of rain falling gently on a metal roof.
25. …having room to breathe.
26. …having a wide margin of error.
27. …a plane landing softly in a storm.
28. …riding on a tandem bicycle.
29. …action.
30. …the interval between periods of sadness.
31. …a scratch for every itch.
32. …travelling.
33. …sharing.
34. …acceptance.
35. …knowing how rather than what.

36. .....considering the grass is greener on one's own side.
37. ...saying 'I can and I will'.
38. ...walking bare-footed in the grass.
39. ...falling autumn leaves.
40. .....a butterfly alighting on one's hand.
41. ...waking up and finding snow against the door on a day off from work.
42. ...Friday.
43. ...a snow fight.
44. ...choice.
45. ...human right.
46. ...freedom of speech.
47. ...dentist being off sick on the day of your appointment.
48. ...singing in the rain.
49. ...falling asleep on the sofa, a good book in your hand.
50. ...not feeling your age.

50 HEALTH QUOTES

1. The man who has health has hope and he who has hope has everything – Thomas Carlyle
2. The wish for healing has always been half of health – Seneca.
3. No disease that can be treated by diet should be treated with any other means – Mamonides.
4. Water, air and cleanness are the chief articles in my pharmacy – Napoleon Bonaparte.
5. The first wealth is health – Ralph Waldo Emerson.
6. Health makes good propaganda – Naomi Woolf.
7. The doctor of the future will be oneself – Albert Schweitzer.
8. Life is a tragedy of nutrition – Arnold Ehret.
9. My own prescription for health is less paperwork and more running barefoot on grass – Leslie Grimutter.
10. A man's health is to be judged by which he takes two at a time – pills or stairs – Joan Welsh.
11. A few germs never hurt anybody – Unknown author.
12. A man with a cough cannot hide - Western Nigeria proverb.
13. Adapt the remedy to the disease – Chinese proverb.
14. After dinner, rest a while; after supper walk a mile - T Cogan.
15. Before healing others, heal yourself – Gambian proverb..

16. Feed a cold, starve a fever – C Morley.
17. Sometimes the remedy is worse than the disease – Francis Bacon.
18. When the mind is at ease, the body is healthy - Chinese proverb.
19. Better to be ten times healed than to be one time dead -Yiddish proverb.
20. If you have nothing to be grateful for, feel your pulse – Unknown author.
21. Be careful about reading health books. You may die of a miss-print – Mark Twain.
22. Eating words has never given me indigestion – Winston Churchill.
23. It is not a question of staying healthy; it is a question of finding an illness that you like – Jackie Mason.
24. I am dying with the help of two many physicians – Alexander The Great.
25. Isn't it un-nerving that doctors call what they do 'practice'? – George Carlin.
26. Never under any circumstances take a sleeping pill and a laxative on the same night – Dave Barry.
27. My doctor recently told me that jogging will add years to my life. He was right. I feel ten years older already – Milton Berle.
28. A hospital is no place to be sick – Samuel Goldwyn.

29. Older people shouldn't eat health foods. They need all the preservatives they can get - Robert Orben.
30. A healthy body outside starts from inside – Robert Urich.
31. The most poetical thing in the world is not being sick – G K Chesterton.
32. The best doctors in the world are Dr Diet, Dr Quiet and Dr Merryman – Jonathan Swift.
33. To live by medicine is to live horribly – Linnaeus, (Carl von Linne).
34. Doctors are men who prescribe medicines of which they know little, to cure diseases of which they know less, in humans of whom they know nothing – Voltaire.
35. The greatest of follies is to sacrifice health for any other type of happiness – Arthur Schopenhauer.
36. I am exhausted trying to stay healthy – Steve Yzeman.
37. I have a healthy body free of the chemicals that once controlled it – Lorna Luft.
38. So many people spend their health gaining wealth and then have to spend their wealth to regain their health – A J Materi.
39. He who cures a disease may be the skillfullest but he that prevents it is the safest physician – Thomas Fuller.
40. He who enjoys good health is rich though he knows it not – Italian proverb.

41. The more you eat, the less flavour; the less you eat, the more flavour – Chinese proverb.
42. The greatest wealth is health – Virgil.
43. It is not food if it arrived through the window of your car – Michael Pollan.
44. As for butter versus margarine, I trust cows more than chemists – Joan Gussow.
45. The physically fit can enjoy their vices – Lord Percival.
46. Most of the food allergies die under garlic and onion – Martin H Fischer.
47. Wine is the most healthful and most hygienic beverage - Louis Pasteur.
48. Any over-indulgence of anything, even something as pure as water, can intoxicate - Criss Jami.
49. Eat healthy, sleep well, breathe deeply, move harmoniously – Jean-Pierre Barral.
50. May your heart be light today – Harley King.

*****

50 WITTY QUOTES

1. Wine is constant proof that God loves us and loves to see us happy – Benjamin Franklin.
2. Get your facts first, then you can distort them as you please – Mark Twain.

3. A successful man is one who makes more money than his wife can spend. A successful woman is one who can find such a man – Lana Turner.
4. God heals; the doctor takes the fees – Benjamin Franklin.
5. Behind every great man is a woman rolling her eyes – Jim Carrey
6. When one is hungry every food tastes good – Unknown author.
7. Vulgarity is no substitute for wit – Lady Violet Crawley of Downton Abbey.
8. Never pick a fight with an ugly person; they have got nothing to lose - Robin Williams.
9. Few things are harder to put up with than a good example – Mark Twain
10. I have never let schooling interfere with my education – Mark Twain.
11. Ninety-nine percent of lawyers give the rest a bad name – Anonymous author.
12. Give me a museum and I'll fill it – Pablo Picasso.
13. If I were two-faced will I be wearing this one? – Abraham Lincoln
14. Don't be so humble. You are not that great – Golda Meir.
15. Everywhere is within walking distance if you have the time – Steven Wright

16. Why don't you write a book that people can read? – Nora Joyce (wife of writer, James Joyce).
17. Show me a sane man and I will cure him for you – Carl Jung.
18. The average person thinks that he isn't – Father Larry Lorenzini.
19. The greatest strength is gentleness – Iroquois proverb.
20. Opportunities multiply as they are seized – Sun Tzu.
21. I would have made a good Pope – Richard Nixon.
22. I don't feel good – last words of Luther Burbank.
23. If you think education is too expensive try ignorance – Derek Bok, Harvard University President.
24. If you lose your temper, you have lost the argument – Anonymous author.
25. Hunger is the best sauce – Anonymous author.
26. Never try to teach a pig a song. It wastes time and it annoys the pig – Anonymous author.
27. Men have become the tool of their tools – Henry David Thoreau.
28. A gentle tongue can break a bone – Proverbs 25: 15.
29. Put a knife to your throat if you have a large appetite – Proverbs 23: 2.
30. Punctuality is the soul of business – Nigerian proverb.
31. Man proposes, God disposes – Nigerian proverb.

32. No condition is permanent – Nigerian adage.
33. Giving money and power to government is like giving whiskey and car keys to teenage boys – P J O'Rourke.
34. The best way to destroy an enemy is to make him a friend – Abraham Lincoln.
35. A day of worrying is more exhausting than a week of work – John Lubbock.
36. Never go to bed mad; stay up and fight – Phyllis Dyller.
37. A lie gets halfway around the world before the truth has a chance to put its pants on – Winston Churchill.
38. If you are too open-minded, your brain will fall out – Lawrence Ferlinghetti.
39. Opera is when a guy gets stabbed in the back and instead of bleeding he sings – Robert Benchley.
40. Once I pulled a job…I picked a pocket on the plane and made a run for it – Rodney Dangerfield.
41. I came from a dangerous neighbourhood. Once a guy pulled a knife on me. I knew he wasn't a professional; the knife had butter on it – Rodney Dangerfield.
42. Sane is boring – R A Salvatore.
43. If only youth knew; if only age could – Henri Estienne.
44. To lengthen thy life, lessen your meals – Benjamin Franklin.

45. I can see him even now going the way of all flesh, that is towards the kitchen – John Webster.
46. As a general rule, the freedom of a people can be judged by the volume of their laughter – Anonymous.
47. A rich man's joke is always funny – Thomas Edward Brown.
48. No wise man ever wished to be younger – Jonathan Swift.
49. It is a good deed to forget a poor joke – Brendan Bracken.
50. The true sign of intelligence is not knowledge but imagination – Albert Einstein
51. Indecision may be or may not be my problem – Jimmy Buffett.
52. Three people can keep a secret only if two of them are dead – Benjamin Franklin
53. It is recession when your neighbour loses his job. It is depression when you lose yours – Harry S Truman
54. Sometimes I wake up grumpy. Sometimes I let him sleep –
55. War does not determine who is right. It determines who is left – Unknown author

50 EXERCISE QUOTES

1. Let exercise alternate with rest – Pythagoras.
2. Lack of activity destroys the good condition of every human being while movement and methodical physical exercise save it and preserve it – Plato
3. Exercise till the mind feels delight in reposing from fatigue – Socrates.
4. It is exercise alone that supports the spirit and keeps the mind in vigour – Cicero.
5. Those who do not find time for exercise will have to find time for illness – Robert de Ferrers, Earl of Derby.
6. Commit to be fit – Unknown author.
7. The only valid excuse for not exercising is paralysis – Moira Northolt.
8. All truly great thoughts are conceived while walking – Friedrich Nietzsche.
9. Walking is the very best exercise. Habituate yourself to walk very far – Thomas Jefferson.
10. Our growing softness, our increasing lack of physical fitness, is a menace to our security – J F Kennedy.
11. Yes, exercise is a catalyst. That's what makes everything happen: your digestion, your elimination, your sex life, your skin, hair, everything about you depends on circulation – Jack Lalanne.
12. Exercise should be regarded as a tribute to the heart – Gene Tunney.

13. There are really only two requirements when it comes to exercise. One is that you do it. The other is that you continue to do it – Jennie Brand-Miller, Kaye Forster-Powell, Stephen Colaquiri and Alan Barclay.
14. Whenever I feel like exercises, I just lie down until the feeling passes – Winston Churchill.
15. Exercise is vulgar; it makes people smell – Y Thornton
16. Exercise is bunk. If you are well you don't need it; if you are sick you shouldn't take it – Henry Ford.
17. The only exercise I take is walking behind the coffins of friends who took exercise – Peter O'Toole.
18. If your dog is fat you are not getting enough exercise – Unknown Author.
19. The only exercise some people do is jumping at conclusions, running down their friends, sidestepping responsibilities or pushing their luck – Unknown Author.
20. I believe that the Good Lord gave us a finite number of heart beats and I'm damned if I'm to use up mine running up and down a street – Neil Armstrong.
21. My idea of exercise is a brisk sit – Phyllis Diller.
22. I consider the refusal to go to the gym as resistance training – Unknown author.
23. Fitness, if it came in bottles everybody would have a great body – Cher.

24. I have to exercise in the morning before my brain figures out what I am doing – Masha Doble.
25. To stay in shape, my grand-mother started walking 5 miles a day when she turned 60. She is now 79 and we don't know where she is – Ellen Generes.
26. A lot of people are afraid of height. Not me. I'm afraid of width – Steven Wright
27. A sweet life is a sweaty life – Toni Sorenson.
28. To get back to my youth I will do anything in the world except take exercise, get up early or be respectable – Oscar Wilde.
29. To feel as fit as a fiddle you must tone down your middle – Unknown author.
30. A feeble body weakens the soul – Jean-Jacques Rousseau.
31. Movement is the best medicine – Donald A Ozello.
32. Life moves for those who move their bodies – Toni Sorenson.
33. Age is only a number. Keep an active life – Lailah Gifty Akita.
34. Exercise is like prose. Yoga is the poetry of movements – Amit Ray.
35. Muscle pain is weakness leaving the body –Tera Lynn Childs.
36. Thinking about working out burns no calories …….. Gwen Ro.

37. There is nothing sweeter than sweat – Lindsey Leavitt.

38. There is no medicine or other intervention that appears to be nearly as effective as exercise in maintaining a person's cognitive abilities – Gretchen Reynolds.

39. So you desire to do nothing? Well, you shall not have a week, a day, one hour free from oppression. You will not be able to lift anything .... – Victor Hugo.

40. ....If you stop exercising physically, your body may not show the result of inactivity for a while but one day you will wake up and find everything is sagging in all the wrong places – Jim George.

41. Exercise is a great leveller. It doesn't matter how rich you are, you cannot buy your way into a great body. You have to do the work – Vinnie Tortorich.

42. Better to wear out than to rust out – 18th century proverb.

43. A fit healthy body; that is the best fashion statement – Jess C Scott.

44. I am so unfamiliar with the gym; I call it James – Ellen de Generes.

45. First it was a dream to lose weight, then it was a goal, then it became a fight, now it is a lifestyle – Fortas Abdeldjalit.

46. Self-delusion is pulling in your stomach when you step on the scales – Paul Sweeney

47. Exercise: You don't have time not to do it – Unknown author.

48. The first time I see a jogger smiling I'll consider it – Joan Rivers.

49. If I'd known I'll live this long, I'd have taken better care of myself – Eubie Blake.

50. Just do it – Nike.

★★★★★

CONCLUSION

Has this book made it clearer to you what laughter is? Does it answer the question: Why do we laugh? Have you gained a better understanding of how laughter sounds are produced and of some of the factors that affect them? It will be most pretencious to claim that those questions have been fully answered.

What is your take concerning the efficacy of laughter as medicine? The jury is still out as far as a definitive answer to this question is concerned.

Are you a Geliophiliac or Geliophobe? (Please refer to Appendix 3). The laughter worshipper in you may be thinking that the day is just round the corner when doctors will prescribe nothing else but 12 belly laughs 4 times a day for obesity; 2 fake laughs every two hours for depression; 4 guffaws every waking hour for congestive heart failure or 3 fake laughs 4 times a day to gain friends and influence people.

Dr Murakami feels so. “One day it won’t be a joke,” he declared, “to see patients sreceive a prescription for a comedy video at a pharmacy for medical treatment.”

If and when this day dawns, what will the laughter dosage be? Will it be by the length of the laughter period, its loudness or its emotional intensity? What will the unit of laughter be called? A ‘geloton’? Or, thinking of the risorious, the laughter muscle, the term could be a ‘risorion’. Therein lies a problem. A laughter meter is still to be invented.

Come on you scientists! Rise up and design a GELOTOMETER or RISORIONOMETER. After all, you designed the pedometer, barometer, sphygmomanometer, thermometer and so many more meters. The laughter meter can transform the assessment of the medical effectiveness of laughter. It can improve the kudos of Gelotology, making it a more precise science. It can curb the propensity of Geliophobes to pour cold water on laughter’s effectiveness as a curer.

In the mean time, let us all enjoy the satus quo - laughter helps us to feel good. It can help us to relax and feel less pain. It can lift depression. It can increase our ability to make friends and influence people. Laughter benefits us; we may not know exactly how. We are patently unable to quantify the amount of the presumed benefits. Still, let’s CARRY ON LAUGHING.

– THE END –

APPENDICES

APPENDIX 1 - TRANSLATIONS OF PROVERBS 17 VERSE 22

Bible Translation	Rendering
King James Version	A merry heart doeth good like a medicine but a broken spirit doeth the bone.
Young's Literal Translation	A rejoicing heart doeth good to the body. And a smitten spirit doeth the bone.
Webster's Bible Translation	A merry heart does good like medicine but a broken spirit doeth the bones.
English Standard Version	A joyful heart is good medicine but a crushed spirit dries up the bones.
New English Ttranslation	A cheerful heart brings good healing but a crushed spirit dries up the bones.
New International Version	A cheerful heart is good medicine but a crushed spirit dries up the bones
New Living Translation	A cheerful heart is good medicine but a broken spirit saps a person's strength.

God's Word Translation	A joyful heart is good medicine but depression drains one's strength.
New World Translation (1984 Edition)	A heart that is joyful does good as a curer but a spirit that is stricken makes the bones dry.
New World Translation (2013 Edition)	A joyful heart is good medicine but a crushed spirit saps one's strength.

APPENDIX 2 - BIBLICAL STATEMENTS ABOUT HUMOUR OR LAUGHTER

(THESE EXCERPS ARE FROM THE KING JAMES VERSION)

1. Genesis 18: 12 – 15 – Therefore Sarah laughed within herself saying: "After I am waxed out and my Lord is old, will I really have this pleasure?" And the Lord said unto Abraham: "Wherefore did Sarah laugh, saying "Shall I of a surety indeed bear a child which I am old?" Is anything too difficult for the Lord? At the time appointed I will return to thee, according to the time of life, and Sarah will have a son."
2. Genesis 21: 6 – And Sarah said: "God hath made me laugh, so that all that hear will laugh with me."
3. Judges 19: 6 – ….. and let thine heart be merry.
4. 2 Chronicles 30: 10 – So the posts passed from city to city through the country of Ephraim and Manasseh

and even unto Zebulun; but they laughed them to scorn and they mocked them.

5. Nehemiah 2: 19 - But when Sanballat the Horonite, and Tobiah the servant, the Ammonite, and Geshem the Arabian, heard it, they laughed us to scorn, and despised us and said: "What is this thing that ye do? Will ye rebel against the king?"
6. Job 5: 22 - At destruction and famine thou shalt laugh: neither shalt thou be afraid of the beasts of the earth.
7. Job 8: 21 - Till he fill thy mouth with laughing and thy lips with rejoicing.
8. Job 39: 18 – When she lifteth herself on high, she scorneth the the horse and his rider.
9. Job 41: 29 – Darts are counted as stubble; he laugheth at the shaking of a spear.
10. Psalm 2: 4 - He that sitteth in the heavens shall laugh; The Lord shall have them in derision.
11. Psalm 37: 13 – The Lord shall laugh at him, for He seeth that his day is coming.
12. Psalm 52: 6 - The righteous also shall see, and fear and shall laugh.
13. Psalm 59: 8 – But thou O LORD shall laugh at them; thou shalt have all the heathen in derision.
14. Psalm 126: 2 – Then was our mouth was filled with laughter, and our tongue with singing; then said they among the heathen, "The Lord hath done great things for them."

15. Proverbs 1: 26 – I will also laugh at your calamity. I will mock when your dread comes.

16. Proverbs 14: 13 – Even in laughter the heart is sorrowful, and the end of it the is heaviness.

17. Habakkuk 1: 10 – And they shall scoff at the kings and the princes shall be a scorn unto them: they shall deride every strong hold; for they shall heap dust, and take it.

18. Matthew 9: 24 - He said unto them: "Give place for the maid nis not dead but sleepeth. And they laughed him to scorn.

19. Mark 5: 40 - And they laughed him to scorn. But when he had put them all out, he taketh the father and mother of the damsel, and them that were with him, and entereth in where the damsel was lying.

20. Luke 6: 21 – "Blessed are ye that hunger now, for ye shall be filled. Blessed are ye that weep now, for ye shall laugh."

21. Luke 6: 25 – Woe unto you that laugh now, for you shall mourn and weep.

22. Luke 8: 53 – And they laughed him to scorn, knowing that she was dead.

23. James 4: 9 – Be afflicted and mourn, and weep; let your laughter be turned to mourning and your joy to heaviness.

- Most of the Biblical references to laughter and humour are in the Old Testament (Hebrew Scriptures)

*****

APPENDIX 3 - SOME PHILIA/PHOBIA JARGON

1. Gelotophilia – Love of laughter (cf gelolotophobia – Hatred of laughter) Alternative terms are Geliophibia and Geliophobia.
2. Coulrophobia – Hatred of clowns.
3. Mephobia – Fear of becoming so awesome that the human race implodes (dies).
4. Nosocomephilia – Love of hospitals.
5. Iatrophilia – Love of visiting the doctor.
6. Belenophilia or Elenophilia – Love of injection.
7. Soceraphilia – Love of parents-in-law.
8. Logophilia – Love of words.
9. Sesquipedalophilia – Love of long words. (Wait for it! A longer word is coming.)
10. Paladophilia – Love of baldness.
11. Cherophilia – Love of gaiety.
12. Choriophilia – Love of dancing.
13. Oenophilia – Love of wine.
14. Arctophilia – Love of teddy bears
15. Tachophilia – Love of speed.
16. Cebophobia – Hatred of food (Anorexia).
17. Doxophilia – Love of being praised.
18. Ergophilia – Love of work.

19. Margeirocophilia – Love of cooking.
20. Didaskaleinophilia – Love of going to school.
21. Enissophobia – Fear of committing an unforgivable sin.
22. Fear of smell or odors – Ofactophobia
23. Kletophobia – Love of stealing (This is a strange one).
24. Gynotikolobomessophilia – Love of kissing a girl's ear lobes. (Can you find a longer philia? Phew! I know one!)
25. Hippopotomonstrossesquipedaliophilia – Love of long words.

APPENDIX 4 SOME LANGUAGE AND SPEECH DISORDER JARGONS

1. Misophonia - Hatred of sound. The term was coined by American neuroscientists, Pawel and Margaret Jastroboff. They also use the equivalent term, Selective Sound Sensitivity Syndrome (SSSS).
2. Aphonogelia – Inability to laugh audibly. It is a very rare condition.
3. Ankyloglosia – To be tongue-tied.
4. Dysarthria – Difficulty in articulating speech.
5. Aphonia – Inability to produce voice.
6. Aphasia – Difficulty to understand and/or produce speech.
7. Echolalia – Meaningless repitition of others' speech.

APPENDIX 6 - LAUGHTER FACTS AND STATISITICS

Listed below are some 'facts' and Statistics about laughter:

1. A child laughs about 300 times a day. An adult laughs about 17 times a day.
2. Among adults, laughter rates peak at about 34 years of age.
3. Most of laughing does not result from jokes but from every day talk.
4. Laughter takes place mostly in groups. Laughter is contagious.
5. The energy needed for 10 minutes of belly laughter is the same needed for 10 minutes on a rowing machine.
6. Three hours of solid laughter (belly laugh) is needed to burn off the calories in a salted packet of crisps.
7. Women laugh more often than men. Women's laughter is softer than men's.
8. People you know sound funnier than others.
9. In Britain in 1960, laughter rate was about 18 minutes per day. In 2013, the rate was about 6 minutes per day.
10. Every week, 35% of people are tickled and 40% of people tickle others.
11. The funniest animal jokes are about the duck.
12. The funniest African animal jokes are about the tortoise.

13. The most ticklish part of your body is the arm-pit.
14. You cannot tickle yourself to laugh.
15. The funniest joke is about 103 words in length.
16. There is no timeless universal joke.
17. Laughter has priority over speech.
18. Laughter is not as contagious as yawning.
19. The brain can tell the difference between a fake and genuine laughter.
20. People can tell over 50% of the time whether or not laughter is fake.
21. Laughter makes people more attractive to others.
22. Laughing first thing in the morning has the same effect as drinking a cup of coffee.
23. Laughter and anger are mutually exclusive.
24. There is a World Laughter Day – the first Sunday of May.

APPENDIX 7 - DEATHS DUE TO LAUGHTER

Name	Date	Circumstances
Zeuxis	5th Century BC	Died laughing at the way he painted the goddess Aphrodites
Chrysippus	3rd Century BC	Died laughing when he saw a donkey eating figs. He then gave the donkey wine to wash down the figs.

Martin of Aragon	1440	This king of Spain died laughing at his own indigestion.
Pietro Aretino	1556	Laughed too much and suffocated.
Thomas Urquhart	1660	This Scottish aristocrat died laughing when he learned that Charles II had taken the Scottish throne.
Wesley Parsons	1893	This farmer in Laurel, Indiana, USA, laughed for two hours over a joke and died.
Alex Mitchell	1975	Died in Kings Lynn, UK while watching the 'Kung Fu Kapers' performed by the Goodies. His wife wrote to thank the Goodies.
Ole Bentzen	1989	This Danish audiologist died laughing while watching "A Fish Called Wanda".
Damnoen Saen-um	2003	A 52-year-old Thai ice-cream salesman, died laughing in his sleep.

APPENDIX 8 - MASSAGE

Massage is the manipulation of superficial and deep structures of the body. The target structures include the skin, muscles, tendons, ligaments and fascia. Also, lymphatic and blood vessels can be manipulated. Sometimes, deep structures like the gut can be manipulated. Massage involves the use of touch and or pressure.

Archaeological evidence has been found that massage was used in ancient civilisations – China, India, Japan, Korea, Egypt and Rome.

HISTORICAL TIME LINE:

From about 3000 BC or BCE (BCE – Before the Common Era).

Egyptian hieroglyphics that date back to the 3rd millennium BCE and depicting massage movements have been found. An example is the drawing of Ankmahor, physician to a pharaoh, using his hand to perform *mass'h*, the Arabic word for massage. Also, paintings, dated to the same period, of massage being practised, were found in a tomb in Saqqara.

In China, Buddhist and Taoists are thought to have created touch as part of spiritual treatment of illnesses. The Buddhist cannon asserts that Buddha's physician, used massage. And, history also shows that a Department of Massage was established later in China's Office of Imperial Physicians.

From about 1000 BCE - Japanese monks took massage from China to Japan and developed Shiatsu from Chinese massage techniques. The primary goal of Shiatsu is to raise the body's energy level and thereby improve the ability of the organs of the body to fight diseases.

800 CE** - In Greece, massage was used to treat athletes before competitions to keep them in peak conditions and after competitions to help them recover from exercise pain and fatigue. Also, Greek physicians used massage techniques to treat various medical conditions. Greek women received beauty treatment through the use of aromatic oils in combination with massage.

The Biblical record suggests that massage was used in the Persian dynasty of the 5th century BCE. It was also in the 5th century BCE that Hippocrates said: "The physician must be experienced in many things but assuredly in rubbing." Sanskrit writings dated around 4th century BCE show that massage was used in India for many centuries previous to that date.

200 BCE- Galen, a physician for many Roman emperors, used massage to treat injuries and physical maladies. Very wealthy Romans received their massage at home, administered by personal physicians, while those less well off, usually victorious gladiators, received their massage in public baths. As Rome descended into moral decadence that led to the final demise of the empire, massage acquired the reputation of being more about the pursuit of carnal pleasure rather than being an avenue for healing.

1700s CE (Common Era – used at time instead of AD which stands for Anno Domini or the Year of our Lord).

Jean Joseph MARIE Amiot and Pierre Martial Gibot, French missionaries in China, returned to Europe and introduced Chinese system of medical massage.

1800s CE - In 1813, the Royal Gymnastic Central Institute opened in Stockholm, Sweden with Per Henrick Ling as its Principal. It was not until 1878 that the Dutchman, Joseph Georg Mezger, a massage practitioner, coined the term "Swedish Massage". He was the first, using French terminology, to classify and describe the five massage techniques stated below.

1900s CE - World War I led to an increase in the use of massage to treat physical injuries. World War II and the polio-myelitis epidemic in Europe and America opened a new chapter for the medical profession. Medical Rehabilitation became a speciality. Massage regained some of its former prestige. However, it has not been able to shed some its seedy past. Massage parlours still exist which surly the profession's noble name. State registration of qualified massage practitioners now take place in many countries, ensuring improved ethical and more holistic practices in the delivery of massage to clients.

The five major strokes of massage are:

- ***Friction*** consists of to and from finger-tip or thumb movements over the skin in treated areas. The pressure exerted may be superficial or deep. The aim of friction is to break down adhesions or so-called knots in subcutaneous structures and to increase the flow of blood to the area.

- ***Kneading or Petrissage*** consists of using the thumb and index finger to lift the skin and the underlying muscles in a given part of the body and then kneading (just like dough), squeezing and rolling the tissues. One hands or both hands may be employed. The purpose served by kneading is similar to that achieved with friction. However, kneading can be used to treat a wider area and deeper structures.

- ***Effleurage*** consists of long superficial "strokes" administered with the palm to warm the skin over an area and then deep "strokes" to promote the flow towards the heart of blood, lymph or excess interstitial fluid. Effleurage is used, in conjunction with elevation, to promote the reduction of swelling in parts of the body, especially the limbs.

  At times, the other massage strokes are preceded by and are followed by effleurage.

- ***Tapotement*** consists of tapping, using the tips of the fingers, drumming or slapping, using the upper parts of the palm or hacking, using small finger (ulnar) aspects of the hands on the skin over the part of the body being treated. The aims of tapotement are to stimulate or excite the nerves over the area being treated and increase blood supply. When excess fluid accumulates in respiratory tracts and lungs, drumming or slapping can be used to loosen the secretions and ease their expectoration.

- ***Vibration*** consists of the application via the therapist's hands of trembling or vibratory motions to an area of the body. The vibrations can be produced by a battery-operated device or massager. Vibration produces stimulation for an area and can facilitated the loosening of excess secretion in the respiratory tracts. This can lead to an improvement in the ability to cough and get rid of the excess secretion.

Up to 36 types and methods of massage have been described.

Of these, the ten most popular are: Swedish Massage, Deep Tissue Massage, Sports Massage, Back massage, Reflexology, Shiatsu, Thai Massage, Hot Stone Massage, Aromatherapy Massage and Pregnancy Massage.

The benefits attributed to facial massage are: Well-being, Wound healing, Reduction in muscle reflex activity (Muscle tension), Reduction in motor neurone activity, maintenance of muscle tone.

ND - #0249 - 080726 - C0 - 197/132/14 - PB - 9781784563431 - Gloss Lamination